A HISTORY OF FIREARMS

A History of Firearms

COLIN HOLCOMBE

.

Colin Holcombe

Dedication

This book is dedicated to the memory of
John Newbury, John Cambridge, Ken Budd and Linda Walden
All four lost their fight against cancer
and have left the world poorer by their absence.

Acknowlegements

I am grateful for the help of
Capt. A Carr ACF formerly of Army Air Corps
and
Former Police Sergeant Stephen Foulkes
of Avon and Somerset Constabulary
in the production of this book.

Second edition 2023

ISBN/SKU: 978-1-3999-6190-5

 Printing, 2023

First edition published 2018

Contents

Introduction

There can be few things that have influenced the advance of societies and their cultures as much as the invention of gunpowder and the development of firearms. As soon as humans began to live in small communities, Possessions as well as the people themselves needed to be defended. What where these defences however? Man has never had talons or fangs to defend himself, so he needed to make a knife or a club, but if he fancied a tasty piece of meat for his dinner, he was hardly going to outrun it. What he needed then was a projectile weapon. A spear, or better still a bow and arrow, and later, the subject of this book, a firearm.

Man's ability to kill his fellow man from a distance and with increasing speed and efficiency moved on from sling-shot and spear, sword and battle-axe, to increasingly sophisticated weapons such as the long-bow and crossbow. But it was undoubtedly the invention of gunpowder that marked the real change and should be the start of our story.

Although gunpowder was first developed, we believe, in 9th century China, the development of weapons using it stalled in China, progressing little further than the fire-lance. It was largely left to the warring nations of Europe, beginning in the 13th century, to bring it to its full potential.

My own interest in such things began at an early age. When I was seven or eight years of age my friends and I were very much into sword-fighting games and my father, who happened to own a large bandsaw, would cut out wooden swords for us to use. The odd scratch or bruise was a small price to pay for the fun we had, and thankfully nobody actualy lost an eye.

Our games inevitably moved on to the wild-west and war games. Remember, this was in the days when, although there was not as much television to view back then, there would be an almost endless choice of westerns to watch every day. The Man from Laramie, Cheyenne, Wells Fargo, Bronco, you name it. We needed guns! and although cap firing toy guns were in abundance then, they were nothing compared to the real gun my father gave me to play with!

Now before you condemn him as a bad father, I feel I should point out that it was an old rim-fire that you could no longer get ammunition for and I was banned from ever taking it out of the house, but the damage was done and I was hooked.

My collection of genuine weapons grew rapidly. Birthdays and Christmas always saw at least one addition to my collection as everybody knew of my interest, so much so that when our elderly next-door neighbour had to go into a home, he presented me with his old army .303.

By the time I was sixteen I had an extensive collection of swords, daggers, bayonets, shields, African spears and some firearms. My firearms firearms included four muskets, my neighbour's .303, two percussion shotguns, two pepper-box revolvers, two percussion pistols, one flintlock pistol, the seven-shot rim-fire that had started it all and a small single shot derringer.

As a teenager I became friendly with a garage owner in Bristol who had not just an extensive collection of guns, but a workshop where he restored them and even built superb replicas. I learnt a great deal from him but sadly lost touch when he moved away.

In deciding what sort of book to write, I looked for inspiration at my own collection of books on the subject, Early Firearms, Antique Pistol Collecting, English Pistols and Revolvers and so on. I realised that the definitive book on the history of firearms has not and probably never will be written. It's far too vast a subject covering a huge chunk of history. Such a work would be a collaboration from a large number of experts and a book of many volumes.

So, I decided to write the book I would have wanted to read when I was first collecting. A book that covers most of the subject in enough detail to give the reader an overview to wet the appetite and will hopefully be an informative and enjoyable read.

The
Early Years

Chapter 1

The Early Years

Gunpowder

Although incendiary and burning substances such as "Greek Fire," that was used by the Eastern Roman (Byzantine) Empire had been used in warfare much earlier, Chinese alchemists are generally credited with the invention of black powder, (sulphur, charcoal and saltpetre,) during the 9th century AD. The grey powder that resulted from the mixture of these ingredients explodes on contact with a naked flame producing a bright flash, a loud noise, white smoke and a strong smell of sulphur.

As early as the 10th century Chinese soldiers were using it for the fire lance, effectively a small cannon on the end of a long stick (Fig 1). This was really little more than a firework and was probably more of a defensive rather than offensive weapon.

Although some sources suggest that the Chinese were aware of the fact that small projectiles such as stones or broken pottery could be fired out of the open end of a fire lance, it would appear that the fire and noise were seen as its chief benefits.

Certainly, nobody climbing a siege ladder would want such a thing in his face.

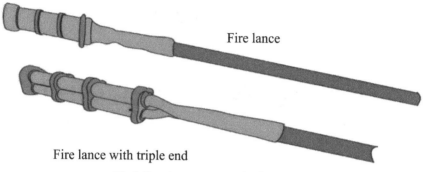

Fire lance

Fire lance with triple end

Fig 1 Two impressions of a fire lance

Development of these weapons however, appeared to stall in China and it was left to the Europeans to develop them further.

Roger Bacon was born in Ilchester, Somerset, around 1220 and died around 1292. He was a philosopher, an alchemist and a Franciscan Friar who studied at Oxford.

Bacon wrote important works on mathematics, optics, alchemy and astronomy and he gave a description of gunpowder around 1250, writing that,

"The powder is enclosed in an instrument of parchment the size of a finger and can make such a noise that it seriously distresses the ears of man and the resulting flash is also very alarming."

It is likely that he learned of the powder from the Arabic or Oriental treaties that he was fond of studying and translating. Although the propulsive force of gunpowder had not yet been fully understood, it is obvious from his writings that he was fearful of the new mixture. There is evidence to suggest that Bacon considered it far too dangerous a discovery to be in the public domain and wrote the formula down only in code.

Warfare at this time was conducted by mounted knights and infantry. The knights themselves looked on personal combat, man to man, as a matter of honour and looked down on the infantry, especially if armed with projectile weapons such as crossbows and longbows, as such weapons were indiscriminate in their choice of target. Combat for the Knight was a trial of strength between individuals, fought with honourable weapons such as the sword and battle-axe which were held in, and aimed by the hand. The eventual winner was the man who had right on his side. There was no honour in striking down your enemy from a distance, possibly even from a place of concealment, as that way even a weak and cowardly peasant could be victorious over a high-born knight.

It was onto that stage that gunpowder made its appearance in Europe in the 13th century and it was with the realisation that the explosive forces produced could be harnessed to propel a missile, that our story really begins.

It is impossible to state with any certainty when the first true gun or cannon was invented or who came up with the idea first, but it is documented that the English used siege guns at the siege of Calais 1346-47, and the earliest depiction of a cannon in an English manuscript dates from 1327 (Fig 2).

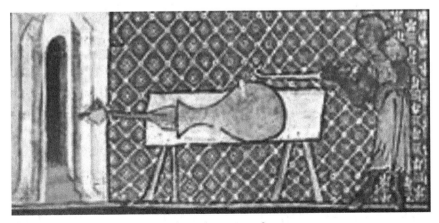

Fig 2. Earliest depiction of a cannon

It shows a vase-like construction that appears to be firing a projectile resembling an arrow. It is possible the arrow was made of metal with a leather wrapping around it to act as a gas seal.

From the illustration there does not appear to be any facility for altering the elevation of the weapon or absorbing any recoil, so it is doubtful that the weapon was any more powerful than a large crossbow.

Gunpowder was a simple mixture of three ingredients, sulphur, charcoal and saltpetre (potassium nitrate,) mixed in approximate proportions 10:15:75. Saltpetre was the ingredient that contained the oxygen which permitted the other substances to burn rapidly, even when cut off from any supply of air. Combustion was very rapid and produced a bright burst of flame when ignited in the open. However, if confined, it produced an explosive force as the gases expanded.

The problem with the early gunpowder was that it burned inconsistently. The ingredients were ground separately and then mixed dry into a substance known as serpentine. This substance was difficult to manage, not least because when being transported by cart in a barrel, the vibration would cause the different components to separate according to their relative density, the sulphur dropping to the bottom and the charcoal rising to the top. This resulted in the need to remix the ingredients at the battery before it could be used.

This problem was overcome shortly after 1400 with the introduction of corned powder. This was manufactured by mixing the ingredients together in water and grinding them into a slurry.

This process ensured that the components remained in a stable mix. After grinding, the mixture was dried into sheets of cake and then wooden hammers were used to break the cake back into grains. After being tumbled to remove the sharp edges, these grains were sieved and separated into coarse, fine and super-fine grains.

Corned powder burned more uniformly than serpentine and resulted in a much stronger powder.

When gunners first began using corned powder they preferred the coarse grains for cannon and the fine grains for smaller weapons and priming. This preference was based solely on experience with no scientific reference, but we now know that the slower burning rate of the large grained powder allowed a larger, slowly accelerating projectile to begin moving slowly as the pressure built gradually, reducing peak pressure and putting less stress on the gun.

It had been realised that gunpowder's force did not act instantly but developed over time, so it therefore worked best when confined in a tubular barrel. Brass and bronze were expensive but wrought iron could be used instead. Construction methods of the time were derived from the art of the cooper, which explains the use of the term barrel being adopted. The wrought iron was shaped around a former, known as a mandrel, and welded together. The tube that was formed was then reinforced with hoops or rings around its circumference.

The 15th century saw the introduction of "trunnions," that consisted of round protrusions on either side of the barrel just in front of the centre of gravity. The introduction of trunnions meant that the gun could be suspended from these and the vertical angle could be easily adjusted.

Sometime before the middle of the of the 16th century a small four wheeled carriage was developed for trunnion-equipped cannon that enabled them to be used effectively onboard ships, first to bombard targets on the land but smaller broadside cannon were soon introduced to fire at enemy ships.

The carriage consisted of two side pieces or cheeks that were joined together with cross pieces known as transoms. The rear end of the cheeks are stepped so that the breech end of the gun could be lifted with iron levers called handspikes and a wedge or "quoin" positioned in order to adjust the elevation. The carriage was fitted with four small wheels that would allow for the recoil when fired and for it to be easily manoeuvered back into its firing position for the next shot (Fig 3).

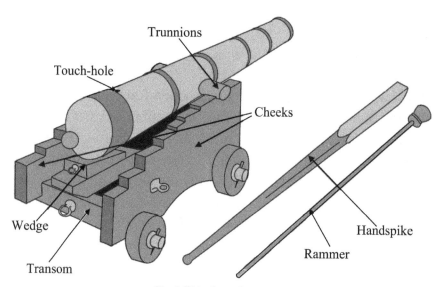

Fig 3 Ship-board cannon

Cannon for use as siege weapons or battlefield artillery had to be transported and set up on site. Some were mounted on carriages with large wheels and were pulled by a team of horses but they were large and unwieldy. The gigantic wrought-iron gun known as "The Dulle Griet" that is still preserved in Ghent has a muzzle thirty-three inches in diameter and weighs 33,606 pounds. The Dardanelles Gun, originally made for the Sultan Mohamet 11 of Turkey in 1454 could, according to tradition, throw a half-ton ball for almost a mile, and at Edinburgh Castle there is "Mons Meg," built in 1449, a drawing of which is seen in Fig 4.

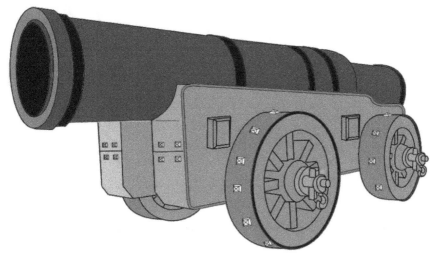

Fig 4 Depiction of Mons Meg

It wasn't until much later, towards the second half of the 15th century, when smaller calibre cannon with large wheeled carriages were introduced that had a tail or trail which rested on the ground during firing. After firing, the trail could be lifted and attached to a two-wheeled carriage known as a "limber." The limber acted as both a pivoting front axle and an attachment point for a team of horses. This could all be achieved without having to dismount the cannon from its carriage, a feature that enabled the cannon to come into its own on the battlefield.

Fig 5 shows an illustration of an early 19th century version of the two-wheeled limber.

Early on, cannon were great for defending or attacking fortifications but were not so useful on the battlefield against an army, as they were far too unwieldy and vulnerable.

What was needed there was not a massive gun that could fire only one shot. It was a smaller gun that could fire several shots at once against an advancing enemy force.

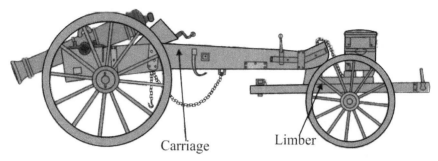

Fig 5 19th century Gun carriage and Limber,

The Ribauldequin was just such a weapon. Consisting of several small-bore barrels laid side by side, either parallel or splayed out like an 18th century ducks foot pistol, it was capable of firing several shots at once, making it an ideal anti-personnel weapon (Fig 6).

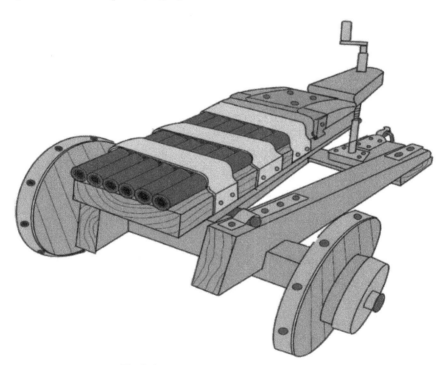

Fig 6 An impression of a Ribauldequin

Possibly used at the siege of Tourni in 1340, its only drawback was the fact that each barrel had to be loaded separately and that would take some time to achieve, time being a commodity that is sadly lacking in the middle of a battle. One way to reduce the amount of time taken loading would be to assigned a man to each barrel and it may have been that notion that led to the idea of each man having his own separate barrel or hand-gun, who knows? Ribauldequins were in use by 1339, and hand-guns were known in Europe by 1350 and at that time, were little more than a ribauldequin barrel fitted to a wooden shaft.

A Flash in the Pan

Chapter 2

A Flash in the Pan

Until the middle of the 15th century small guns or hand-guns differed from larger cannon only in size. Fig 7 shows an early hand-gun or hand-cannon dating from 1424 and as can be seen, they were basically a small cannon mounted on the end of a stick or pole. The pole was necessary because the metal would quickly become too hot to hold in the hand.

Fig 7. Hand-cannon 1424.
Metropolitan Museum of Art

They still needed one person to hold and aim the weapon and another to touch off the priming charge but things were about to change. The thing that changed it all was the introduction of the slow match.

The slow match was a cord or length of twine that had been soaked in a solution of potassium nitrate and dried.

When lit, the end of the match would smoulder in a slow and controlled way. All that was needed then was a means of allowing the person holding and aiming the gun to also apply

the smouldering end of the match to the touchhole, and thus
eliminate the need for a second person.

The Matchlock.

The solution was easy, a simple shaped arm called a serpentine that held the end of the match and could be operated by
the same man that was holding the gun.
At first, the serpentine was attached to the side of the stock
by means of a central pivot. The upper end had jaws that could
hold the end of the smouldering match and when the bottom
of the serpentine was lifted, the match was brought down into
contact with the touchhole. Fig 8.

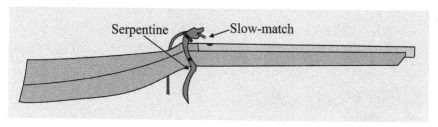

Fig 8: Early matchlock with serpentine pivoted on the outside of the stock

The touchhole itself had a small depression surrounding it
so as to centre the match and help bring the end of it into
direct contact with the hole. It is impossible to say exactly
when the first matchlock was used but it was probable sometime around 1440.
The first real improvement to this set-up was the migration
of the touchhole to the side of the barrel, enabling the gunner
to sight along the top of the weapon. With the touchhole now
at the side of the barrel, a small pan was needed to contain the
priming powder and this flashpan could be fitted with a hinged
cover to protect the powder from wind and rain until the gun
was to be fired.

Not long after its introduction, the serpentine was replaced by an internal mechanism operated by an external lever or trigger, and the people most suited to make such a mechanism were the locksmiths of the time. Hence, the firing mechanism of a gun has always been known as it's lock.

The matchlock mechanism, (Fig 9), consisted of a serpentine on the outside that had a clamp to hold the smouldering match, secured in place with a threaded screw. Inside, a lever or sear pivoted on the inside of the lock plate and linked to the serpentine in such a way that when its hindmost end was raised the serpentine was made to swing in a circular motion, bringing the lighted end of the match down upon the flash-pan. As the trigger or firing lever was pulled, the far end of the sear would be pushed up at A in Fig 9, causing the front-end B to move down and rotate tje tumbler.

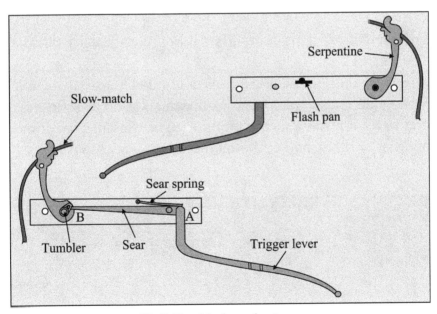

Fig 9: Matchlock mechanisum

By the earl 16th century the matchlock had proved its worth on the battlefield, reputedly killing 8,000 cavalrymen at the battle of Pavia in 1525.

Further advances in design included a trigger mechanisum, whereby the spring powered serpentine was cocked and released by a trigger, Fig 10. The disadvantage of this mechanisum however, was that there was a danger of the match being extinguised if snapped too hard into the priming pan.

Fig 10: Matchlock musket with trigger and trigger guard
Royal Armouries Collection

Later, towards the end of the 17th century the priming pan and cover was included in the lock mechanisum, and the English matchlock musket differs little from the early flintock that replaces it.

Some Non-Europian countries continued to use the matchlock much longer than their European counterparts. In India and Japan for example, it continued to be used in one form or another until the end of the 19th century. Figs 11 and 12.

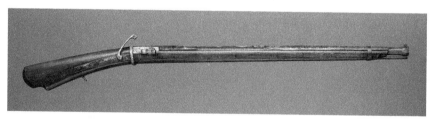

Fig 11: Japanese matchlock late 17th century
Metropolitan Museum of Art

Fig 12: Indian matchlock mid 19th century
Metropolitan Museum of Art

Loading and firing a matchlok was a hazardous business. The first thing the shooter or musketeer had to do when re-loading was to remove the match and hold it in his left hand, keeping it well away from any gunpowder during the loading process. It is possible the musketeer would keep both ends of the match smouldering so that he could light one end from the other if one went out during firing.

Holding the musket upright with the butt resting on the ground he next poured a measured amount of coarse powder from his bandolier, that hung from a belt at his waist, into the end of the barrel.

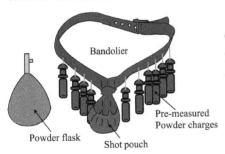

Fig 13: Musketeer's bandolier

Next, he placed a fragment of wadding and a ball taken from his pouch and rammed them home with the ramrod taken from its slot in the musket's stock. The wadding was used to form a gas seal between powder and ball,

With the gun loaded he could now return the match to the serpentine and place some fine priming powder in the pan. The pan would often have a sliding cover to protect the priming powder from the elements until firing. The piece was then ready to be fired.

The matchlock had many drawbacks, not least of which was the need to keep adjusting the length of the match as it burned down and the fact that a source of fire was needed in case the match went out. It was also a tricky process having to handle both gunpowder and a smouldering match whilst loading. Unfortunate accidents must have been a frequent occurrence.

What was needed was a means of igniting the charge without the need for fire or matches. It was most probably German ingenuity that solved the problem and paved the way for future developments with the invention of the wheellock around 1530.

The Wheellock.

With the wheellock, the priming powder in the flashpan was ignited by mean of a spark, generated by a piece of iron pyrites connecting with a serrated wheel that was rotated by means of a powerful mainspring.

Once the gun was loaded with powder and shot in the same way as the matchlock, the wheel was turned clockwise by fitting a key over the squared end of the central spindle. Turning the wheel in this way wound up a short chain that connected the inside of the central spindle to the free end of the mainspring.

After approximately three-quarters of a turn, a sear (or scear), fitted on the inside of the lock-plate would engage in a notch or "bent" on the edge of the wheel, securing it in place with the chain wound around the spindle and the mainspring bent.

Next, the flashpan, which had the serrated edge of the wheel protruding slightly through it at the bottom, was primed with fine powder.

The pan cover was then slid in place and the dog, holding the iron pyrites, or later flint, lowered to rest on top. The dog is held in place by its own spring (Fig 14).

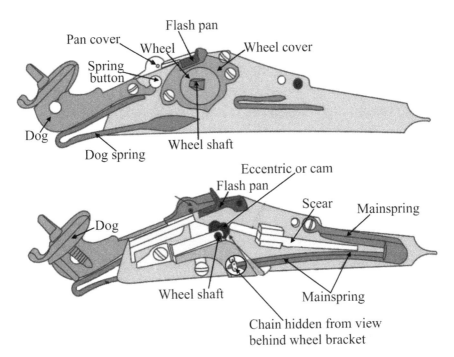

Fig14: The Wheellock mechanisum

When the trigger is pressed it draws back the scear horizontally, freeing the wheel to rotate. At the same time, a cam attached to the spindle draws back the pan cover, allowing the iron pyrites in the dog to contact the turning wheel, generating a shower of a sparks and igniting the priming powder. Fig 15 shows a fine example of a wheellock.

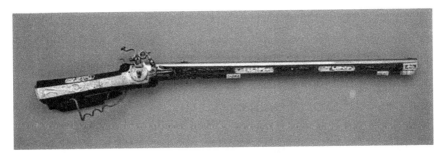

Fig 15: A beautiful example of a German wheellock
The Metropolitan Museun if Art

No one knows who or where the wheellock was invented, although it does seem to have originated in an area between Nurnburg in southern Germany and Milan in northern Italy. There has been speculation that it was invented by Leonardo da Vinci, but we shall never know for sure who came up with the idea first.

What we do know is that it had a huge impact on society. Here was a gun that could be ready to fire and carried concealed, and gave rise to the first gun control laws and the birth of the pistol.

The invention of the wheellock had far reaching affects well beyond just the introduction of the pistol. The fact that a charge could be set of without needing a slow match or other sourse of fire, meant that it could be triggered from a distance by pulling a string, or by springs or clockwork. The booby trap was now a possibility.

Other developments included the first cartridge. In the 16th century this was simply a tube of rolled paper containing enough powder for one charge.

All the shooter had to do was bite off one end, pour a small amount of powder into the pan and the rest down the barrel, the ball would follow and the paper as a wad, before being rammed down the barrel.

The development of the cartridge decreased the time it took to load, as well as ensuring that less powder was spilled.

Although the wheellock was rugged and reliable, it was never suitable to be an infantry weapon. It was expensive to manufacture, and required a separate spanner to wind the wheel. This eccessory could easily be dropped in the heat of battle, rendering the weapon useless, and for these reasons, the matchlock remained the principal infantry weapon in Europe.

The Snaphaunce

The snaphaunce differs from the wheellock inasmuch as the sparks are generated by the flint striking a steel, rather than being in contact with a rotating wheel. It first puts in an appearance towards the second quarter of the 16th century. The snaphaunce is a somewhat simpler mechanism than the wheellock but nevertheless the wheellock was reliable and still remained a popular personal weapon.

Its name probably originated because the action resembled that of a pecking rooster. It became known as the schnapp-hahn or pecking cock, and when it arrived in England the Dutch schnapp-hahn became corrupted to to snaphaunce, and the vice that held the flint soon became known as the cock.

In order to load and prepare the snaphaunce for firing, the main charge and shot are rammed down the muzzle of the musket with the ramrod and the pan is primed with fine powder from the shooter's powder horn, Fig 16.

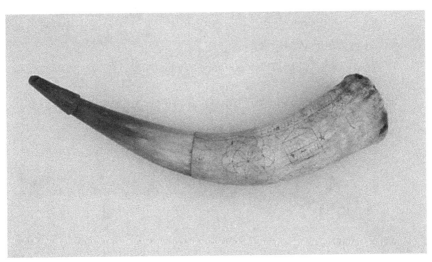

Fig 16: Powder horn
Metropoliton Museum of Art

The pan cover is then closed and the cock pulled back to a "set" position. When the trigger is pulled the scear is withdrawn horizontally through the lock plate freeing the cock, which is forced down upon the steel by the action of the mainspring, Fig 17.

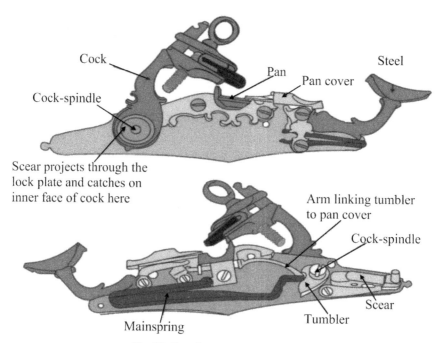

Fig 17: Snaphaunce mechanisum

Fig 18 shows a fine example of a snaphaunce pistol c 1655.

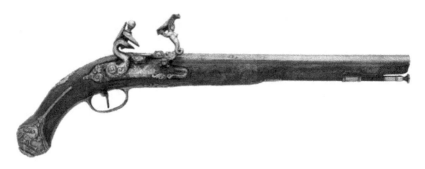

Fig 18: Snaphaunce pistol c 1655

The Dutch where a great trading nation, and their ships carried the Snaphaunce all over the Mediterranian, the Baltic, and influence the design of firearms in England, Scotland and the Scandinavian countries.

In many of these countries, when they began to make there own fireams, they copied the lock they were familier with. In Morocco for instance the snaphaunce was still being made as late as the 1880s, centuries after it had stopped being manufactured in the land of its birth.

The Scandinavian Lock

From the mid-sixteenth century to the mid-eighteenth century there existed a variant of the Dutch snaphaunce.

With the Scandinavian lock, Fig 19, the sear passes through the lock-plate to engage the tail of the cock. The mainspring is on the inside of the lock-plate and presses down onto the tail of the tumbler. The pan cover, that has to be opened manually before firing, is separate from the steel. There is no half-cock safety position but the weapon can be made safe by turning back the steel.

On later examples, dating from the second half of the 17th century, the steel can be turned to one side to provide a safety position. As with the English lock, later forms of this lock have a tumbler with notches or bents and the scear engages with those rather with the tail of the cock.

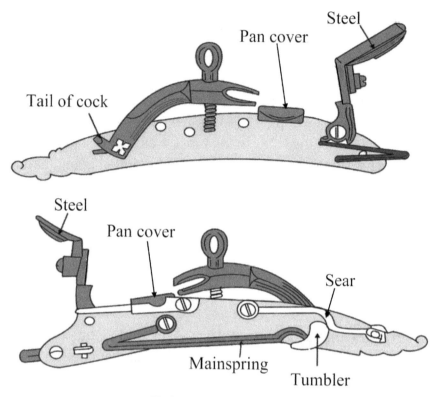

Fig19: Scandinavian lock

The English Lock

During the first half of the 17th century a lock appeared which incorporated many of the features of the snaphaunce, but in this lock, the pan cover is combined with the steel. This combined steel and pan cover or "frizzen," consisted of a hinged cover working upon a screw set in the lock-plate and held in position by a small spring. From the back of the pan cover a curved steel rises at such an angle as to produce sparks as the flint strikes it in a scrapping action. The pan cover spring performs the dual roles of holding the pan cover in place until the moment of firing and also of ensuring that the steel offers sufficient resistance to create sparks when struck by the flint Fig 20.

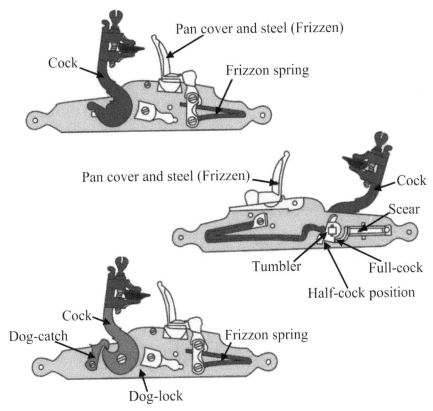

Fig 20: Early 17th century English lock and dog-lock

This simpler mechanism dispensed with both the sliding pan cover and the link connecting it to the tumbler, but meant that a safety position for the cock had to be devised so that the gun could be carried primed and loaded, without the danger of a premature discharge.

This safety mechanism consisted of a half-cock position from which the gun could not be fired. The scear passed through the lock plate and engaged the tail of the cock in the full cock position but engaged in a notch or bent in the tumbler, inside the lock plate when half-cocked. In addition to the half-cock position, some guns had the additional safety of a small catch in the form of a hook on the outside of the lock-plate. This hook engaged in a notch on the back of the cock when drawn back just beyond the half-cock position and had to be pulled back by the thumb before the piece could be fired. The hook on these pieces was called a dog catch and the guns with this feature became known as dog-locks, shown in the bottom illustration of Fig 20.

In the later form of the lock, dating from around the time of the English Civil War, the scear no longer penetrated through the lock-plate but engaged in two bents cut into the tumbler.

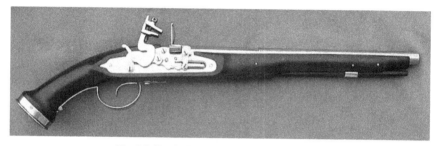

Fig 20: English civil war dog-lock pistol

This lock wasn't in production for long however, as it was quickly superseded by the French flint-lock.

The Mediterranean Lock

There are basically two versions of this lock, sometimes referred to as a Miquelet, which are the Italian and the Spanish, both of which have horizontally acting scears and both of which were developed during the first half of the seventeenth century. The Italian lock is shown in Fig 21, where the sear (or scear) consists of two arms positioned at A and B. The front arm A, provides a half-cock position by engaging the toe of the cock, while the back arm, B, hidden behind the heel in the illustration, provides the full-cock position by engaging with the heal.

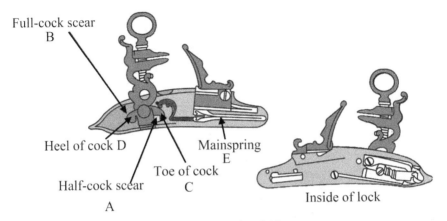

Fig 21: The Italian lock

When the trigger is pulled, both arms of the sear are withdrawn horizontally through the lock plate allowing the cock to descend under the pressure from the mainspring pressing on the toe.

The Spanish lock differs from the Italian inasmuch that both arms of the sear pass through the lock plate in front of the cock Fig 22. The toe of the cock in this lock ends in a blade B. The half-cock is provided by a stud C and the full-cock by a flat blade D.

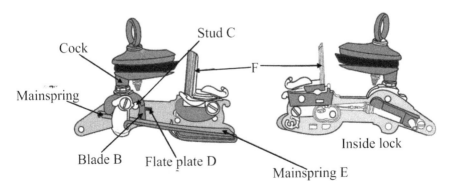

Fig 22: The Spanish lock

In later versions the stud C is often replaced by a second blade. Unlike the Italian lock, the mainspring E presses up against the heel of the cock. With early versions of this lock the face of the battery or frizzen, has vertical grooves and can be removed and replaced when it becomes worn. Fig 23 shows a pistol which is a fine example of the Spanish lock.

Fig23: A Spanish flintlock pistol
Metropolitan Museum of Art

The French Lock

The main difference with the French lock that appeared in the early 17th century was the fact that the sear operated vertically rather than horizontally. Two bents or notches are cut in the tumbler at the half-cock and full-cock position and the scear engages with them, rather than passing through the lock-plate and engaging with the cock itself. The operation of the sear is the only real difference between the English and the French locks, although the dog-catch is seldom seen on the French lock, which gradually became the standard for all Northern European locks Fig 24.

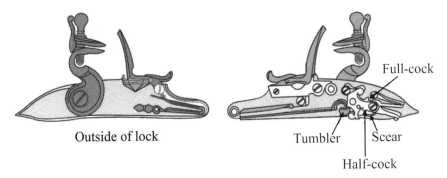

Outside of lock

Full-cock

Tumbler | Scear

Half-cock

Fig24: The French lock

The English soon adopted the French vertically-acting scear and applied it to their own locks, which already had the one-piece frizzen, and by 1700, every major power was using a version of the French lock.

Each nation had its own variations, with differing bores for the barrels and different styles of decoration, but in one form or another, the French lock dominated the battlefields of the world until the beginning of the 19th century.

The French infantry musket of 1717, often referred to as the Charleville musket, with a smooth bore barrel of .69 inch (17.5mm) calibre. became the standard French musket until 1840. The barrel was 46 inches in length and was pinned in place, but it also had a single metal band around the centre and four iron pipes that held the ramrod. The overall length of the musket was 62 inches and it weighed approximately 9lb.

Fig 24 shows how a pinned barrel was attached to the stock. The pin passed through an escutcheon plate on the side of the fore-stock and then through a metal lug attached to the underside of the barrel.

The illustration shows just one wedge pin but most long guns would have had two or even three in some cases.

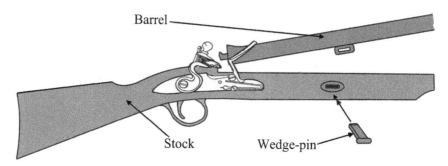

Fig 24: Pinned barrel and wedge pin

In 1728 the pinned barrel was replaced with one held by three metal bands, making it far more secure when the bayonet was used. In today's army, the bayonet is viewed very much as a last-ditch weapon but in the 18th century the bayonet played a far more prominent role and accounted for possibly as much as a third of all battlefield casualties, Fig 25.

Fig 25: A French Charleville Musket c1777

The lock of the musket was also revised, with a longer frizzen spring and a slightly modified cock design. More minor changes took place later, such as replacing the wooden ramrod with a steel one but it was essentially the same gun.

The musket was redesigned again in 1763 with a 44-inch barrel, a reshaped butt and a ramrod with a slightly flared end. Although shorter in length overall it was slightly heavier than its predecessor. This increase in weight proved unpopular so the weapon was made lighter three years later with a thinner barrel wall and a slimmed down stock. The end of the ramrod was once again altered, this time to a button shaped end.

Between 1770 and 1776 various small changes took place such as stronger barrel bands and a modified ramrod retaining spring.

In 1777 the stock was redesigned again, this time with a cheek rest on the inside of the butt, a slanted brass flashpan and a trigger guard with two rear finger ridges. This was the musket used during the French revolution and the American war of independence.

Most of the infantry model muskets described above would have been available in shorter versions for officers and dragoons after 1754. These versions were some 10 inches shorter than the infantry model. In addition, there was a navy version of the 1777 model that was of similar length to the dragoon model but was fitted all brass furniture, a common feature of naval weapons. The French musket was so successful that copies of it were made in Russia, Holland, Austria, Belgium and Prussia.

Its main rival was the British Land Pattern Musket, affectionately known as "Brown Bess". There were several derivatives of the basic pattern including the Long Land Pattern, the Short Land Pattern, the India pattern, the New Land Pattern and the Sea Service Pattern, two of which are shown in Fig 26. All were muzzle loading smooth bore muskets of .75 calibre.

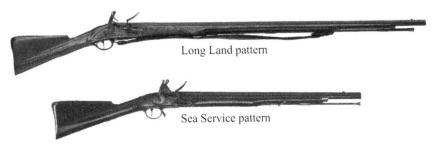

Long Land pattern

Sea Service pattern

Fig 26: Long Land pattern musket (Brown Bess) and Sea servive pattern
National Museum of Scotland

The nickname Brown Bess is often linked to Queen Elizabeth 1, but the dates don't support the theory, Elizabeth 1 having died in 1603. However, it is likely that the brown came from the artificial browning of the barrel that was supposed to help prevent rusting and to avoid glair in bright sunlight. There are reports that the soldiers themselves disliked the browning and polished it off, feeling that the dull appearance of the weapon did not go well with their bright scarlet coats and gleaming buttons. The Land pattern musket was in service from 1722 until 1838 when it was superseded by a percussion weapon.

The Bayonet

I mentioned earlier, very briefly, about the important role that the bayonet played on the battlefield, so I feel I should say a little about its development. The name "bayonet" is believed to have been taken from the place that it first appeared, Bayonne, in southern France. This may or may not be the case but we do know that daggers from that area were called bayonets in the 1500's.

At first these bayonets were simply daggers with tapered handles that could be driven into the muzzle of gun. Obviously, there were some major drawbacks to early bayonets being fitted in this way. Firstly, the gun could not be used while they were in place. Secondly, once they had been used, having been driven into the body of some unfortunate enemy soldier, they could be jammed too tight in the barrel to be easily removed, and thirdly, if they were not rammed in hard enough to start with, they could be left in the body of the ill-fated victim when the musket was withdrawn. Despite their deficiencies however, some English and French regiments were issued with them in the third quarter of the 17th century.

The advantages however, of having a weapon that could be used both at a distance and in hand to hand fighting, meant that attempts were soon made to improve bayonet design. Hoops were attached to the hilt that would loop over the barrel, but this wasn't very successful. It was towards the end of the 17th century that the far more dependable socket bayonet was developed and adopted throughout Europe.

The socket bayonet consisted of a short sleeve that fitted over the barrel and was locked in place with a stud and slot. The triangular blade was offset from the sleeve by an elbow piece that kept it clear of the muzzle. Every soldier could now be both musketeer and pike-man. Fig 27

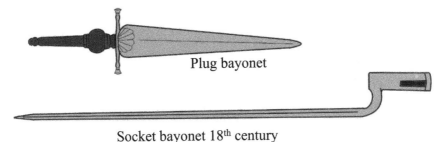

Plug bayonet

Socket bayonet 18th century

Fig 27: Drawing of a Plug Bayonet 17th centurey above and below an 18th century Socket Bayonet.

The Blunderbuss.

It was usual for a line of soldiers to fire a volley of shots at an advancing army and as this was found to be such a successful tactic, it was a natural progression of thought to conclude that a single gun firing a volley would be useful for an individual in certain circumstances. Gunsmiths produced small arms along the same lines as the ribauldequin with multi barrels, but these were expensive and it was not an easy matter to ignite several charges from a single lock, although the ducks-foot pistol was produced in some numbers, Fig 28.

Fig 28: Flintlock duck-foot pistol c 1220

The natural conclusion was to design a gun that would fire a number of projectiles from a single barrel.

A larger bore to accommodate more shot and a wide flaring muzzle seemed to be the obvious answer and the blunderbuss was born, Fig 29.

Fig 29: Early flintlock blunderbuss with wide flaring muzzle

There is a myth that the early blunderbuss, with its very wide flaring muzzle, could be loaded with almost anything, broken glass, sharp stones and even nails, but this is highly unlikely. If a nail or piece of metal was caught crosswise in the barrel it could prove disastrous for the shooter. The manuals of the time call for the gun to be loaded with musket or pistol balls or buckshot.

It was soon discovered that the spread of shot did not depend on the flare of the muzzle, as originally thought, but more on the bore of the gun at the breech, the length of the barrel and the uniformity of the bore expansion from breech to muzzle. Eighteenth century gunmakers came to recognise this after 1750 and started producing shorter, large calibre arms with almost cylindrical bores Fig 30.

Fig 30: Blunderbuss c 1700
Metropoliton Museum of Art

The blunderbuss proved a very popular weapon and when properly used was a very effective arm for defending a home, or for repelling boarders from enemy ships. Stagecoach guards were also fond of them because the flared muzzle made it easier to load on a swaying stagecoach and the sprayed out shot meant that you had a greater chance of hitting your target.

The development of gun locks went hand-in-hand with the development of the gunstock, resulting in proper grips and an enlarged butt. At first the straight stocks, that were popular in Germany, were held against the cheek with the butt resting on the shoulder but the French developed a sharply curved butt that rested against the breastplate of the firer. As the power of firearms increased however, the sense of bracing the butt against the shoulder to absorb the power of the recoil was soon appreciated.

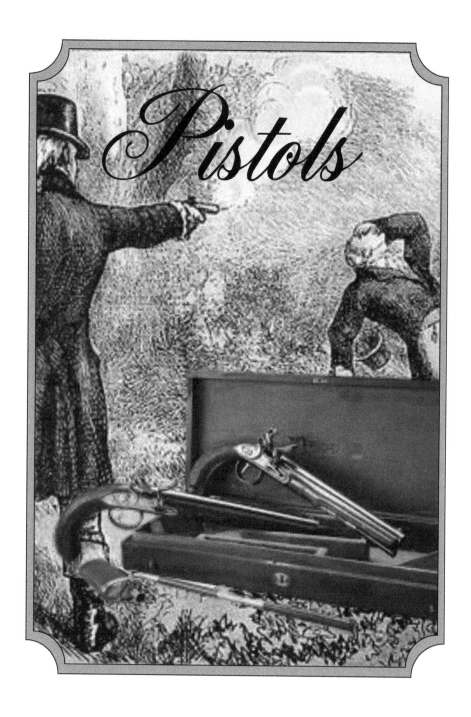

Chapter 3

Pistols

Pistols of the 17th and early 18 centuries tended to have long barrels, which allowed the slow burning powder sufficient time to accelerate the bullet to full velocity before it exited the muzzle. To compensate for the increased weight of the barrel, a gradually sloping butt with a heavy end was required, Fig 31.

Fig 31: Flintlock pistol with slopping butt and heavy end

Long barrelled pistols of this type were produced in England, Flanders (Liege), Germany (Bohemia), Austria, Holland and Italy. The countries of origin of these pistols can often be identified, both by the style of any decoration and by the proof-marks. After around 1720 however, there was a tendency for the barrel length to be reduced from around fourteen inches down to twelve or even 10 inches Fig 32,

Fig32: New Land Pattern pistol

It was around the middle of the 17th century that a completely new kind of pistol appeared.

This new pistol had a barrel that screwed off for breach loading. The barrel was shaped like a miniature cannon and was in two parts, consisting of a fixed breech, ending in a cup shaped to receive a ball and the barrel proper, which was attached to the breech by a screw thread. These new pistols became known as turn-off or cannon barrelled pistols Fig 33.

Fig 33: 17th century turn-off or cannon barrelled pistol

To load the new gun, the barrel had to be screwed off to expose the breech cup. There was an opening at the bottom of the cup through which the chamber could be filled with powder. A ball, of slightly larger diameter than the bore of the barrel, was then placed in the cup and the barrel screwed back into place.

Because the ball was slightly larger than the bore, a spanner was needed to tighten the barrel, which had a small lug on it to engage with the spanner. This method of breech loading took longer than muzzle loading but had the advantage of ensuring a more accurate and powerful shot. Fig 33a.

Fig 33a; A spanner is needed to tighten the barrel

With muzzle loading guns the ball used was slightly smaller than the bore of the barrel so that it could be rammed down easily. This meant that some of the force from the exploding gases escaped around the side of the ball. It also meant that the ball was free to wobble slightly as it travelled the length of the barrel, resulting in less accuracy. The actual direction of shot would depend to some extent on the last bounce the ball took before leaving the muzzle. With the cannon barrel, the ball was slightly larger than the bore, resulting in no loss of power and a more accurate shot, especially if the barrel was rifled, as they frequently were.

There is a report that as Prince Rupert, nephew of King Charles 1 and his cavalry leader during the English Civil War, halted at Stafford on September 13th 1642. The prince drew one of his screw-barrelled pistols and fired at the weather-cock of St. Mary's Church, some one hundred and eighty feet from where he and King Charles rested. The bullet pierced the tail of the cock and the King was astonished, calling it a lucky shot, whereupon the prince drew his other pistol and repeated the shot, hitting the cock a second time.

Guns of the cannon barrelled design that were intended for use on horseback, were fitted with a swivel mechanism attaching the barrel to the gun, which prevented the barrel being dropped during the loading process Fig 34.

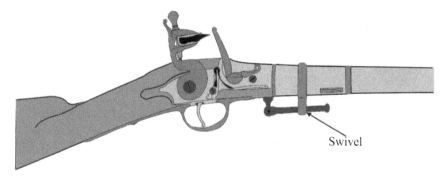

Swivel

Fig 34: Cannon barrelled carbine with swivel c 1720

The powder of the day was slow burning and a long barrel was needed to give it time to fully ignite before the ball left the muzzle. Because the ball fitted tightly in the cannon barrelled pistol, the forward force exerted was delayed for a fraction of a second, enabling a shorter barrel to be used. In turn, the shorter barrel made the gun easier to keep in a purse or pocket, making it the weapon of choice for any civilian who needed protection from robbers and highwaymen.

The pocket pistol proved so popular in fact that it was quickly refined. 17th century screw barrelled pistols had a separate lock-plate the same as the muzzle loaders, but in the eighteenth century the lock-plate and the breech chamber were cast as one, and these guns tend to be referred to as Queen Anne pistols or Box-lock pistols.

The lock mechanism was moved inside which meant that only the cock and frizzen protruded above the centre of the barrel, making it easier to withdraw from the pocket in an emergency situation. Placing the lock inside also lessened the amount of wooden stock needed, reducing the bulk of the gun even further. Another innovation was the introduction of a folding trigger that only popped down when the gun was cocked, Fig 35.

Fig 35: 18th century pocket pistol with lock plate and chamber cast as one.

Duelling Pistols

Duels have been fought with almost every weapon you can think of since early times, but the weapons most commonly brought to mind are of course, the sword and the pistol.

Swords were the preferred weapon of gentlemen until the third quarter of the 17th century when the duelling pistol took over.

Early duels with firearms were fairly informal affairs and the guns used could be whatever the duellist owned or could get hold of, but gradually rules and etiquette evolved. The most usual duel was an affair in which the duellists faced each other at a distance of some ten or fifteen paces. The experienced duellist would stand side on to his rival and keep the arm not holding the pistol behind his body, so as to present the narrowest target and he would fire as soon as he took aim.

Duelling became so commonplace that special pistols were developed. The specialised duelling pistol had to be accurate and well balanced. It was often the case that the custom or rules of the duel precluded deliberate aiming, and in any case, there was seldom time and the man who fired first had a considerable advantage, if his shot was on target. This meant that that the pistol should be so balanced that it would point at the target almost automatically when raised.

French duelling pistols were usually rifled, that is to say they had spiral groves cut into the interior of the barrel to impart spin to the bullet and make it more accurate. English pistols were not rifled, as custom frowned on it. However occasionally, an English pistol can be found with blind rifling, that is rifling that stopped short of the muzzle to give the impression of being a smooth bore. Before you say anything, I know! I thought the English were the nation of fair-play as well.

The barrels are usually about ten inches long and octagonal on the outside, and they would have been browned or blued to avoid glare. Avoiding glair was considered important, so the decoration on the gun, if any, would have been of iron or steel and finished in the same way as the barrel. Fig 36 shows a typical English flintlock duelling pistol.

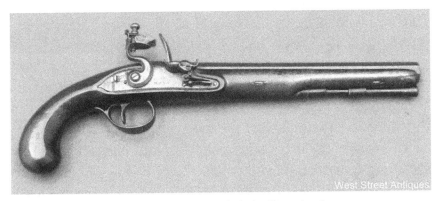

Fig 36: A typical English duelling pistol
West Street Antiques

Duelling pistols, as any other fine guns, would have been made in pairs and be fitted into a plain felt or velvet lined box with all its accessories.

Fig 37 shows a pair of duelling pistol by Durs Egg in their original box.

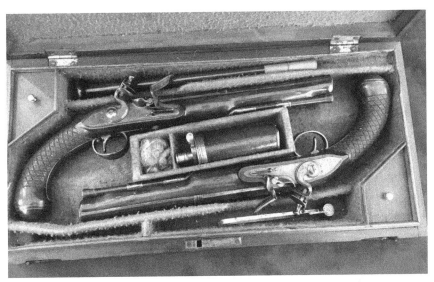

Fig 37: Boxed duelling pistols by Durs Egg of London

The Hair-trigger

Later duelling pistols can also be seen with hair-triggers. These triggers had a screw adjustment so they could be set to the individual preference of the user.

The trigger itself consisted of two parts pivoted upon the same pin, A and B in Fig 38.

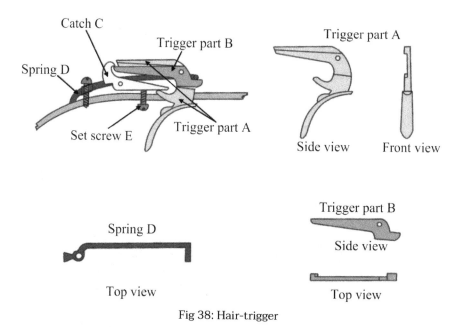

Fig 38: Hair-trigger

Part A resembles a common trigger and can be used as such if the hair-trigger is not set. The second part B is a simple lever, the front part of which, in front of the trigger, is pressed down by a powerful spring D.

To set the trigger, part A is pressed forward and that in turn presses the arm of lever B down until it engages in the catch C, which is operated by a light spring not shown in the diagram for clarity. Now, even slight pressure on the trigger will release the catch causing the longer arm of the lever to fly up as the short arm is pressed down by the spring. This action will be passed on to the trigger, causing it to strike the sear and fire the pistol.

The set screw E, can be screwed up or down to adjust the amount of pressure required to release the catch.

Pistols fitted with hair-trigger also had a "detent," a small guide pivoted on the tumbler and designed to prevent the scear from catching accidentally in the half-cock position and preventing the gun from firing. The addition of the detent was necessary because the hair-trigger did not exert a steady pressure on the sear, as did the usual trigger, but delivered a sharp light blow to the tail of the sear that was just sufficient to free it from the full-cock bent and release the tumbler.

Tests carried out in the nineteen-sixties found that an English pistol of c1790 could hit a man-sized target, three times out of four over a distance of eighty-five yards.

Possibly the most elaborate duel in history took place in France in 1808. The dispute was between M. de Grandpre and M. le Pique and concerned a certain Mademoiselle Tirevit of the imperial opera, who apparently was unable to choose between her two suitors. On their orders two identical balloons were constructed, and on the day of the duel, the two men entered the baskets of their respective balloons, along with their seconds.

The balloons were released some eighty yards apart from the grounds of the Tuilleries, watched by a large crowd. The gentlemen were to fire, not at each other, but at their opponent's balloon, and each was armed with a blunderbuss. When they reached a height of about half a mile the signal was given from the ground to fire.

Le Pique fired first but somehow managed to miss completely. De Grandpre on the other hand, scored a direct hit, collapsing Le Pique's balloon and sending it, together with Le Pique and his unfortunate second to the ground. De Grandpre landed some miles away and hastened to the arms of Mademoiselle Trievit, whose mind was now, presumably, made up.

Later advances in Flintlocks

One improvement that is seen in pistols made after 1780 is the addition of a small roller bearing at the point where the pan cover spring presses on the pan cover itself. This allowed the lock to operate more quickly by reducing the friction at that point Fig 39.

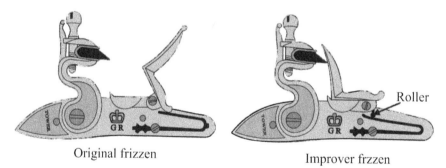

Original frizzen   Improver frzzen

Fig 39: Inproved frizzen

After 1800, the pan, instead of being hollowed out in the middle of a broad flat surface, has a sharp rim like the edge of a spoon. This enabled the pan cover to fit much better and it is often referred to as the rain-proof pan.

Another improvement was a change in the way the main-spring interacted with the tumbler. Previously, the end of the main-spring ended in a hook that pressed directly onto a notch or step in the tumbler, but now the end of the spring was connected to the tumbler by means of a steel arm or swivel, greatly reducing the amount of friction Fig 40.

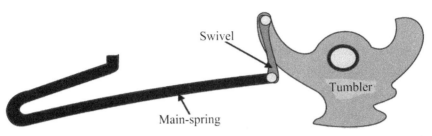

Fig 40: The end of the spring was connected to the tumbler by means of a steel arm or swivel

Probably the biggest improvement was perfected by English gunmaker Henry Nocks.

One problem had always been that the priming charge only ignited one side of the main charge in the breech and ignition spread slowly to the rest of the charge. The latter part of the 18th century saw attempts made to deliver the flame from the priming pan to the centre of the main charge by way of a long channel but this resulted in too many misfires.

To try and overcome this problem a new kind of breech plug was invented. Previously the end of the breech had been closed with a simple screw plug (Fig 41, top left).

The new breech plug had a centrally located hole or chamber, the bottom of which was connected to the touch hole by a narrow passage known as the anti-chamber. In this way, the jet of flame resulting from the ignition of the priming powder was delivered directly to the centre of the main charge (Fig 41, top right).

This resulted in greatly improved combustion and consequently, a faster rise in pressure and a greater missile velocity.

Unfortunately, there was a price to pay. The new system meant, paradoxically, that there was more of a time lapse between pulling the trigger and the discharge of the gun. Gunmakers were dismayed, but the benefits of the new system were far too important to be ignored.

Henry Nock designed a breech plug with only a short channel and a large anti-chamber for an ignition charge. The anti-chamber was connected to the main breech chamber by a narrow opening so that on ignition the powder in the anti-chamber, burning quickly because of its confinement, issued a jet of flame into the main chamber and ensured immediate ignition of the main charge (Fig 41).

The ingenious Nocks also provided a clean-out screw for easy cleaning of the breech.

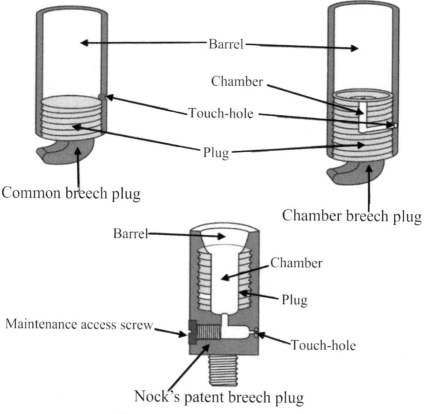

Fig 41: Nock's pattent breech plug

Because the explosive forces developed much more quickly, Nock's patent breech enabled barrels to be shortened, making the guns much lighter in weight, and it was as a result of this, that side by side double-barrelled guns became practical.

The Scottish Pistol

Somewhere we have to look at the very distinctive Scottish pistol and this seems as good a place as any. Many Dutch arms had been imported into Scotland during the sixteenth century so it is natural that when the Scots started to produce their own weapons in the late sixteenth century they copied the arms with which they were most familiar.

The Dutch mechanism was adopted completely but the Scottish craftsmen looked to their own Celtic traditions for design and ornamentation, something that makes the Scottish pistol so instantly recognisable. The Scottish gunsmiths seemed to have an aversion to trigger guards for some reason and although this was not a problem in the time of the snaphaunce, when the steel could be pushed forward to make the gun safe, when the French mechanism was adopted the exposed ball trigger was a considerable hazard. See Fig 42.

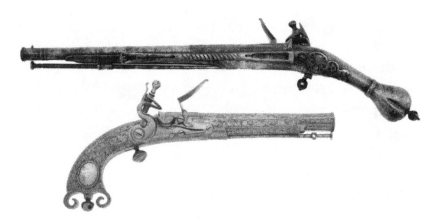

Fig 42: Two examples of distinctive Scottish pistols

The earliest snaphaunces sometimes had wooden stocks with brass or silver mounts but even then, there were the all metal stocks that became a Scottish characteristic. The butts were shaped to resemble ram's horns, lemons, fish tails and crowns and often in the centre would be screwed a metal pricker for cleaning out the touch-hole if it should become clogged.

There was a lack of suitable timber in Scotland for making gun stocks which accounts for there being such a large percentage of all metal construction. The centre of manufacture of Scottish pistols seems to have centred around the village of Doune in Stirlingshire.

Doune was located at an intersection of roads used by cattle herders to take their cattle from the Highlands to Stirling and other major cities, and many Highlanders would buy their goods in Doune on their way back to the homes. Firearms, mostly made by continental manufacturers, were some of the items available in the Doune markets.

In 1647 however, a refugee Flemish blacksmith named Thomas Caddell settled in Doune and although a blacksmith by trade, he saw an opportunity and soon began to make pistols as well and soon acquired a reputation for making fine arms and his pistols were purchase by a large number of Highland officers during the 1730s and 1740s. Later pistols are also found made of brass or bronze and highly decorated.

Allegedly, a pistol made at Doune was the first weapon fired in the American War of Independence, often referred to as "the shot that was heard around the world."

The manufacture of pistols at Doune appears to have stopped in the early 1800s.

Under the Hammer

Chapter 4

Under the hammer

The Forsyth detonating system

Alexander John Forsyth was a Scottish minister born in 1768. His two main interests, apart from the church one supposes, were science and hunting waterfowl. Like others who shared his interest in bird hunting, the flintlock frustrated him. No matter how little time elapsed between pulling the trigger and his gun discharging, the birds seemed quicker.

The noise of his firearm wasn't the problem, it was the flash in the pan, the light from which would warn his prey of danger long before ball or bullet would reach its target.

At first the young minister tried to hood or shield the flash with some moderate success but it was not good enough. He needed a method of ignition that would not send a massive warning signal to his prey.

He had heard of experiments with new kinds of powder and priming agents. Fulminates, are salts produced by dissolving metals in acid, and they explode when struck violently with a hammer. It is unknown who first discovered the explosive qualities of fulminates but the diarist Samuel Pepys mentions fulminate of gold in 1663.

Claude Louise Berthollet, a French chemist, tried unsuc-
cessfully to substitute fulminate of silver or potassium chlorate, for the saltpetre in gunpowder during the late 1700s, and
Edward Howard was working along similar lines in England.
Neither of these gentlemen however, thought of using one of
the explosive fulminates to actually set off a charge.

Forsyth at first simply replaced the powder in the pan with
fulminate. Sparks would set of the fulminate, but it was not as
reliable as gunpowder. Next, he tried setting it off with a sharp
blow. This worked better than a spark but often failed to set
off the main charge. The open pan was just not suitable. He
needed to find a way to confine the fulminate in a small space
and direct the flame into the breech.

He succeeded in 1805 with his "scent bottle lock." This
consisted of a magazine of the detonating compound at one
end and a striker at the other, Fig 43.

Fig 43: Pistol with Forsyth's percussion lock
The Royal Armouries Collection

The whole lock pivoted around a cylindrical plug that was
attached to the breech of the gun. By rotating the lock, a
measured amount of primer was deposited in a small cavity
situated on the upper surface of the plug.

Returning the lock to its firing position isolated the magazine from the cavity and lined up the striker with it. Fig 44.

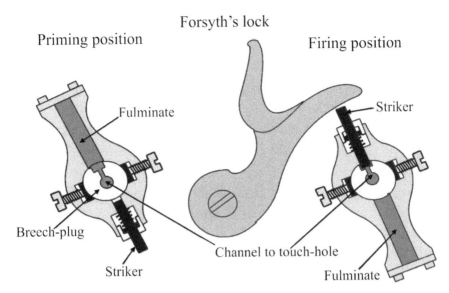

Fig 44: Forsyth's scent bottle lock

When the trigger is pulled and the hammer falls, the striker sets of the compound in the cavity and the resulting flame is channelled into the main charge in the breech through a vent or touch-hole.

After extensive testing, Forsyth took his lock to London and showed it to Lord Moira who was the Master of Ordnance.

Lord Moira was impressed with both Forsyth and his new lock and saw definite military potential in it. He asked Forsyth to take a leave of absence from his Aberdeen Presbytery and work at the Tower of London where a workshop and work force would be provided for him.

Unfortunately, the first few months did not go well and the one official trial of the new gun was disappointing. A new master general was appointed and Forsyth's association with the government ended.

Forsyth was disappointed but undaunted, and with the help of a good friend, James Watt of steam engine fame, he applied for and obtained a patent covering the use of fulminate as a primer for firearms.

With a patent under his belt, Forsyth formed a partnership to manufacture and sell his guns.

The new lock was extremely successful. The only drawback was the sensitive nature of the detonating powder and the possibility of an accidental detonation of the powder in the magazine.

Great care was taken in the manufacture and fitting of the lock, and the plug, around which the whole revolved, was coated with platinum to resist wear and corrosion.

Two small brushes of cork were fitted inside the primer upon either side of the pan or priming cavity to prevent the flash from the pan reaching the magazine. These brushes were held against the plug by two small set-screws.

As a further precaution, a small hole was drilled through the lid of the priming magazine. This hole was filled with a plug of horn or cork, so that if the primer in the magazine should explode, the plug would be blown out without offering enough resistance to cause the pressure to damage the magazine itself.

Another advantage of the Forsyth system was that it was easy to convert flintlocks to the new system. Indeed, it has been estimated that more guns were converted to the new system than were ever made from scratch.

Although Forsyth's detonating system was very successful, it nevertheless had a relatively short life because of the arrival of the percussion cap.It is perhaps surprising that Forsyth himself, once he had developed his lock, never considered any approach other than using fulminate as a loose powder.

The Percussion Cap

The first step towards the introduction of the percussion cap was the patch primer, where the fulminate was sandwiched between two pieces of paper. These patches were stuck to the face of the hammer and exploded against a hollow nipple at the breech.

There were also pill or pellet locks. The charge was fired by means of a small pellet of compound that was either mixed with Gum Arabic or some other binder and rolled into little pellets that were inserted into a touchhole and struck by a sharp pointed hammer.

There was also the tube lock. This consisted of a soft metal tube filled with fulminate, one end of which was inserted into a touchhole while the other rested on an anvil ready for the hammer to strike. Joe Manton patented the first English tube lock in 1818 but others also claimed credit for it.

All these systems had the advantage of doing away with the use of loose detonating powder.

Fig 45: Percussion caps

The pill lock in particular enjoyed considerable support both on the continent and in America, although it never really caught on in England.

The system that really took over was the percussion cap Fig 45.

Nobody knows who first came up with the idea of the cap. There are many claimants however, including Joseph Egg, Joseph Manton and John Purdey, all notable gun makers. All we know for sure is that the first patent was granted to Francois Prélat in 1818, but he was not the inventor.

One other possible inventor was Joshua Shaw, who emigrated to America in 1817. He claimed he had been unable to obtain a patent in England because of Forsyth's patent on fulminate locks. Shaw could not obtain an American patent until he had lived in the country for three years but for some reason that he never explained, he actually waited five years before applying in 1822 and by that time there were several patents in Europe. All that can be said with certainty is that the cap appears to have been first used in England between 1818 and 1820.

Whether Shaw's cap or Manton's or one of the others mentioned, it consisted of a thin metal casing of copper in the shape of a miniature top hat. Inside at the bottom of the cavity, an amount of fulminate of mercury or potassium chlorate was covered with a piece of tin foil and sealed with a drop of shellac to keep it waterproof.

In use, the cap was positioned over a hollow nipple that led directly to the charge in the breech. When the hammer struck, a spurt of flame was directed straight into the main charge, and so long as the main charge was kept dry the gun could be fired, even in driving rain Fig 46.

Fig 46: Pistol that would used the new percussion cap
Andrew Bottomley Antique Arms and Armour

Sportsmen claimed that the new percussion guns did not shoot as forcefully as the flintlock. Advocates of the new system pointed out however, that the new guns shot faster, so it wasn't necessary to aim as far ahead of a flying duck.

In the end, the new guns won out and the flintlock era came to an end, although the military in England retained the flintlock in service until about 1842.

It was in 1842 that the brass mounted, smooth bore Tower pistol with its 12 bore nine-inch barrel, Fig 47, superseded the cavalry flintlock pistol.

Fig 47: Cavalry brass mounted Tower pistol 1843
Kings Shilling Antiques

In 1856 the rifled Enfield pistol appeared, Fig 48. . This had a ten-inch barrel and a sight, but unfortunately it came too late, as the single shot pistol was now regarded as obsolete by the authorities. The advent of the percussion cap meant that it was possible to produce a reliable compact revolving pistol.

Fig 48: Enfield military pistol with sight 1856
J. C. Militaria

One of the first gunmakers in America to adopt the new percussion cap was a Philadelphia gunsmith by the name of Henry Derringer Jr. Derringer had been making military rifles for the United States government but when he switched to the new percussion system in 1825 he began to concentrate on pistols. Fig 49.

Fig 49: Derringer pistol c 1830
Jerry Bernal. Collectors Firearms

As was the case in Europe, respectable citizens, as well as thieves and the somewhat less respectable, carried pistols as a matter of course, and the smaller of Derringer's guns suited them well,

The typical Derringer was between four and nine inches in length and calibres ranged from .33 to .51. They were not accurate over any great distance but across a bar or gaming table they were lethal, and disagreements between armed men were common place.

It was also a Derringer that John Wilkes Booth used to assassinate Abraham Lincoln as he sat in his box at Ford's Theatre on Good Friday 1865.

Also in America, Edward Maynard patented a system which could prime a percussion musket automatically and in 1855, the US army replaced its smooth-bores with a rifled musket featuring Maynard's system. The system consisted of a roll of coiled tape with small, evenly spaced caps or pockets, similar to those used in a toy cap-gun, and these pockets were filled with mercury fulminate.

This roll of "caps" was fed out of a magazine by means of a serrated cog-wheel that rotated as the gun's hammer was cocked. The nipple was constructed so as to take a regular percussion cap if Maynard's tape was unavailable, Fig 50.

Maynard's new system still required the musket's powder and ball to be loaded conventionally into the barrel, but the tape system meant that the percussion cap no longer needed to be manually loaded onto the percussion lock's nipple. This saved the soldier a step during the reloading process, which increased his overall rate of fire.

Confederate President Jefferson Davis, was so enthusiastic about the design that it was installed on the Springfield Model 1855 rifle-musket.

The Maynard tape worked well under controlled conditions but proved to be unreliable in the field. The mechanism was delicate and fouled easily. The tape had been advertised as waterproof, but this proved not to be entirely true. The paper strips were susceptible to adverse weather and even humidity. It was also possible for two or even three caps to detonate together.

For later muskets, like the Springfield Model 1861, the army returned to the traditional percussion cap.

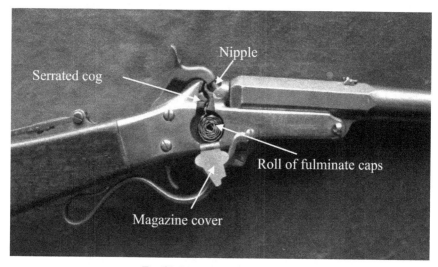

Fig 50: Maynard's cap system

Fig 51: A Maynard Carbine

Although Maynard's percussion system with its roll of caps, eventualy proved too unreliable for military use, his legacy lived on. Even as late as the nineteen sixties it was possible to purchase a roll of Maynard caps, not for detonating a a real charge, but for supplying a realistic sound effect for countless top guns. I myself can remember purchasing rolls of caps that came in a small cardboard box with the name Maynard on the top. Fig 52

Fig 52: Toy gun from the 1960s clearly showing the Maynard roll of caps.

The Spinning Ball

Chapter 5

The Spinning Ball

No one really knows why or when rifling began to be used in firearms, but it would seem from surviving examples that sporting guns with rifling were in use as early as the middle of the sixteenth century, and there is no reason to suppose that these examples were the first such guns.

As to why, some people have speculated that the grooves were originally intended to collect the fouling from inside the barrel, but there is very little to support such an unlikely theory. It is much more likely that the grooves were cut deliberately to set the ball spinning before it left the barrel, as for years the feathers of arrows and crossbow bolts had been set at an angle so that they would spin in flight. It was known that a spinning arrow was more stable in flight, and it is almost inevitable that a curious gunsmith would consider whether the same would apply to a round projectile from a gun.

Whoever it was who first tried it out would have had no idea why the spinning ball flew straighter or struck harder. We now know that there were two reasons. First, to make them easier to load, smoothbore muskets were loaded with a ball that was of a smaller diameter than that of the barrel, which meant that the ball bounced around as it travelled the length of the barrel and the direction it travelled when leaving the muzzle depended, to some extent, on its last bounce. To be affected by the rifling, a ball fired from a rifled barrel had to be a snug fit, resulting in it always left the muzzle travelling in a straight line.

The second reason was that a musket ball was never perfectly round and the density of the metal was never evenly distributed, so the centre of gravity was never at the centre of the ball, and this would cause it to wobble in flight. When the ball spins, it evens out the weight differences and creates an artificial equilibrium.

Although the reasons for it were not understood until much later, seventeenth century shooters were quick to recognise the superior performance of rifled barrels.

The problem was that, in order for the groove to impart spin to the ball, the ball had to be a tight fit in the barrel and that made loading difficult. To load a tight fitting ball, it was necessary to hit it into the barrel to start, either with the end of the powder flask or a small wooden mallet and then drive it home with the ramrod. Ramrods were usually made of wood that would sometimes break under the strain and striking the ball into the end of the barrel could knock it out of shape, lessening its accuracy.

The problems were partially overcome by using a slightly smaller ball and wrapping it in a greased patch of leather or cloth. This way, it was the greased patch that was forced into the grooves and imparted the spin to the ball. Although extra time was used when loading, in order to wrap the ball in the patch, it was easier to ram the load down the barrel and the greased patch also helped to clean out fouling from the barrel.

The Flintlock rifle was a short gun as a rule, between three and four feet in length, but they were often large calibre, .75 not being unusual. The barrels were octagonal with a slight flair at the muzzle and deep multi-grooved rifling. Most had a box carved into the right side of the stock with a sliding cover where a shooter would carry his tools, patches and extra flints.

This was the standard rifle of central and northern Europe at a time when many were seeking new opportunities in a new land across the Atlantic. Once they arrived in the new land, many pushed inland from Philadelphia to the frontier to establish new communities in the wilderness, and they took their rifles, and their gunsmiths, with them.

Life on the frontier was unlike anything they had known at home. Conditions were different and there was a greater variety of game. The rifle, that had largely been an instrument for sport, was now a vital tool for survival.

Changed conditions led to changes in the rifle to make it more useful in its new environment. Calibres were reduced to conserve powder and shot and barrels were lengthened, both to improve accuracy and to ensure that all the powder burned while the ball was in the barrel. Indigenous woods were used for the stocks, although the multi-grooved octagonal barrel, blued to eliminate glare, and the same sights were retained.

The changes had made it a long graceful gun that was very accurate, and also America's first contribution to firearm development. These changes didn't take place overnight, but by 1750 the true American rifle had evolved. Many names have been given to the American rifle over the years, and it's been called the "long rifle" the "Tennessee rifle" and the "Kentucky rifle, Fig 53.

Fig 53: Kentucky rifle

No matter what the new rifle was called, it was an important item in any household and every man on the frontier became proficient in its use. Boys learned to shoot as soon as they were big enough to hold a long rifle, and by the age of twelve, they were expected to play their part in putting meat on the family table and take their place beside the men in times of attack by hostiles.

Despite being commonplace, marksmanship with the rifle was much admired, and recreation often took the form of shooting matches. One of the most common forms of match being the "Turkey shoot," with live birds tethered behind a log. The idea was to induce a bird to raise its head and then shoot it, the first man to do so won the bird.

It was the American Revolution that would be the first test of the American rifle as a military weapon. In June 1775 the Continental Congress authorised ten companies of riflemen as a first step towards creating a national army, and the next day appointed George Washington as commander-in-chief. The army was formed, and in the beginning, it was made up entirely of riflemen.

Major George Hanger of the British Army, and an excellent marksman himself, is quoted as saying, "provided an American rifleman were to get a perfect aim at 300 yards of me, standing still, he most undoubtedly would hit me, unless it was a very windy day..." Hanger was of the opinion that the American rifle was the best in the world, and that the American rifleman was the best shot.

Despite its accuracy however, the American rifle lacked some of the things necessary in a military arm. It required a marksman to reap the benefit of its accuracy, and a regular in-fantryman with a smoothbore could get off three shots in the time it took a rifleman to load and fire once. The other serious drawback was its lack of a bayonet for hand-to-hand fighting. Washington ordered his riflemen to carry folding spears for just such an occasion, but also cautioned his company commanders never to let his riflemen be caught in a place where they could not run to safety.

The musket was undoubtedly the workhorse of the revolution, but the performance of the rifle did not go unnoticed. European countries that did not have regular riflemen added them to their armies, and those that already had some, added more. The British lagged somewhat behind in adopting an official rifle, but extensive trials were carried out by the Ordnance Board at Woolwich and in the end, the board selected an English gun made by Ezekiel Baker of Whitechapel, London.

The Baker rifle Fig 54, was not the most accurate rifle tested, but shot well at ranges up to two hundred yards or more and this was judged to be good enough for military use as there were other features that made it suitable. The grooves in the barrel made only a quarter turn and this not only reduced the amount of fouling that would collect, it also made it easier to load.

Fig 54: The Baker rifle 1805

The ball for the Baker rifle was just small enough to drop down the barrel under its own weight. With the patch it would take the rifling, without it, accuracy would be sacrificed but the rifle could be loaded at least as fast as a musket, which was a considerable advantage in the closing stages of an engagement when visibility would be reduced by smoke. The Baker rifle also had one other feature that made it an ideal military weapon - it could be fitted with a bayonet. The bayonet for the Baker rifle was longer than usual to make up for the relatively short length of the rifle itself, and became known as the sword bayonet for obvious reasons Fig 55.

Fig 55: The Baker rifle sword bayonet

Once the rifle was selected, volunteers were requested to form a Corps of Riflemen, and then one battalion of the new 95th regiment, which quickly became known as Rifle Brigade. A second battalion was formed in 1805 and to distinguish this elite band from the rest of the army, a new green uniform was introduced.

The new Rifle Brigade gave a good account of itself against the armies of Napoleon in the Peninsula War, where tales of heroism and personal and group exploits abound.

When the war in Spain ended, six companies of the Rifle Brigade were dispatched to America, where Britain and America were at war. They arrived just in time for the Battle of New Orleans, the only occasion when the American rifle and the Baker rifle would oppose each other on the same battlefield.

The battle was not a long drawn out affair, indeed, the main engagement was over in little more than two hours. Estimates of the British dead and wounded range from two to three thousand, while the American count is put at six to seven hundred. The real tragedy however was the fact that the main battle took place on January 8th 1815, and a treaty, effectively ending the war, had been signed in far off Ghent on 24th December 1814. News travelled slowly back then.

The main problem with the muzzle loading rifles was the time it took to load. Smoothbore muskets were quicker to load because the ball didn't have to fit as tightly. In France, Captain Gustave Delvigne decided that the only way to speed up loading would be to load a loose ball and then make it fit tighter once it was in the breech. To this end he designed a rifle with a small cavity at the breech. The ball, when loaded, would rest against the cavity and two or three taps with the ramrod would flatten it sufficiently to be a tight fit. Although the system worked to the extent that it made the ball a tighter fit, it also distorted the ball's shape and made the weapon inaccurate.

Colonel Thouvenin of the artillery, produced a rifle with a stout pin, half the diameter of the bore and projecting from the breech. During loading, the powder filled the space around the pin which served as an anvil and once again the ramrod was used to flatten the bullet, the end of which was cupped to lessen the distortion. Thouvenin had switched from using a spherical ball to an elongated projectile but this did not fully solve the problems.

Various other systems were tried, but the breakthrough came with a different idea altogether. Captain John Norton is often credited with having experimented with expanding bullets in 1823. The idea was that an elongated bullet should have a cavity in the base and that the force of the charge itself would cause the bullet to expand to fit the bore and take spin from the rifling, but his idea was not taken up.

In France, Captain Delvigne also decided that a loose fitting bullet with a hollow base would be expanded by the force of the charge and fit the bore tightly, but it was another Frenchman who would give his name to the system of gas expanding projectiles.

Claude Etienne Minié refined the shape of Delvigne's bullet, and in 1849 he added a small iron cup designed to be driven into the base of the bullet on discharge, thus ensuring a uniform expansion on all sides. The cup however, was found to be a hazard, sometimes parting from the bullet and leaving the muzzle separately and endangering other soldiers in the vicinity. It was also found to be unnecessary.

The British determined that a slightly redesigned bullet worked well without a cup, although they backtracked somewhat and added a boxwood plug anyway. If nothing else, it did help to prevent any damage occurring to the bullet before loading. At the same time the Americans reached the same conclusions. James Henry Burton, Assistant Master Armourer, designed a bullet that needed no plug of any kind, and it was quickly adopted by the government.

It was Burton's bullet design, and one can only speculate as to how irked he was, that the Americans insisted on calling it a "Minié Ball," after Claude Minié.

It is of no consequence but interesting to note that, Delvigne, who first looked at the possibility of an expanding hollow-based bullet, receives no credit in the public's mind for originating the system. Burton and the British designer who produced projectiles that actually saw use are seldom mentioned. Minié, on the other hand, whose system was defective and only saw experimental use, became a familiar word in America.

The development and adoption of the new bullet effectively put an end to the smoothbore musket. The rifle could now be loaded quickly and every soldier could be supplied with an accurate weapon.

In Great Britain, the first rifles to use the new bullet were little more than rifled versions of the smoothbore muskets of 1842, but the .72 calibre proved too large for the elongated bullet so a new Enfield rifle was adopted the next year. A new, Royal Small Arms Factory was set up at Enfield, and who should be appointed chief engineer, none other than James Henry Burton.

The Enfield rifle and short Enfield rifle were excellent weapons and started to appear on battlefields around the world by 1856. Fig 56.

Fig 56: The Enfield rifle

The Americans were a little slower in approving guns for the new bullet but in the end adopted three, a long rifle, a short rifle and a pistol with a detachable shoulder stock. A characteristic of the American arm was the tape primer patented by Edward Maynard, described in chapter four and shown in Fig 50. The Maynard system had its problems however and later models abandoned it in favour of the conventional percussion cap.

There were some other developments and changes, especially to target pieces, but no great new innovations were to follow until the appearance of the modern cartridge. Advances in machinery had reduced the cost of cutting the grooves in the barrels, which meant that there was no longer an economic reason to choose a smoothbore over a rifle, so the smoothbore was assigned to history and the rifle ruled supreme.

Loading at the Breech
and
The Modern Cartridge

Chapter 6

Loading at the
Breech and the
Modern Cartridge

The development of the modern cartridge goes very much hand-in-glove with the perfection of breech loading systems, as will be seen.

Gun makers and inventors had tried from early times to load from the breech end of the barrel but there was a big problem in doing so.

It meant that the barrel would have to have an opening at both ends, and the opening at the breech end would have to be sealed quickly, and more importantly, tightly, to prevent flame and gases escaping and causing, not just a loss of power, but injury to the shooter.

Breech loading cannon had appeared as early as the first quarter of the fifteenth century. There were two systems, both involving a completely separate breech. One was like a short tube itself, just long enough to contain a charge of powder, closed at one end and slightly tapered at the other so that it could slot into the breech end of the cannon's barrel.

Once in position it was locked in place with a wedge or key. Other systems involved a breech that could be unscrewed. The screwed breech would have been fine for smaller cannon, but I imagine trying to screw a large heavy breech in and out would have been a trial, Fig 57.

Breech loading cannon

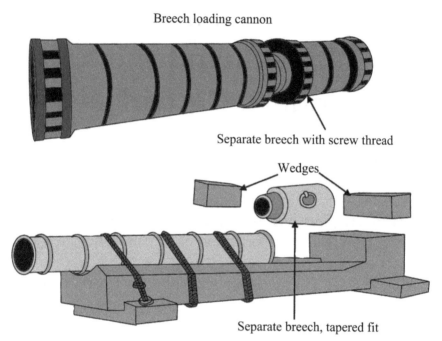

Separate breech with screw thread

Wedges

Separate breech, tapered fit

Fig 57 : Breech loading cannon

Breech loading small arms came later but were still relatively early in our story. Fig 58 for instance, shows an early breech loading snaphaunce pistol circa 1650.

These guns used a separate iron tube rather like a modern cartridge to contain the charge. The breech was hinged so that it could be broken open for the tube to be inserted, and then closed and latched once the charge and shot was in the chamber.

Fig 58: Italian breech loading snaphaunce circa 1650
Nationl Firearms Museum

Over the next hundred years or more all sorts of breech loading systems were dreamed up, among them was the idea of a screw in breech plug but there were various problems. The screwed plug could be difficult to screw back in again, especially in the heat of battle. Fouling could also impede re-screwing the plug, or the plug itself could be dropped.

It was well over a hundred years before a French engineer named Isaac de la Chaumette revived the idea in 1704. His idea, like most good ideas, was simple.

With Chaumette's gun, the plug screwed all the way through the barrel from top to bottom and the bottom of it was attached to the trigger guard. The trigger guard then acted as a handle for screwing and unscrewing the plug, and if the plug became difficult to screw back in, it provided the necessary leverage. Chaumette's idea of taking the plug all the way through the barrel, also meant the plug no longer had to be fully removed for loading, because unscrewing it from the bottom, opened up a hole at the top through which ball and shot could be loaded Fig 59.

As a Huguenot, Chaumette fled to England in 1721 where he obtained a Royal patent, much to the dismay of English gun makers who tried hard to break his control of the system. One of his licensees, with the possibly unfortunate name of

Bidet, manufactured an improved version of the gun with a quick-acting thread that dropped the breech plug to the loading position with just one turn of the trigger guard.

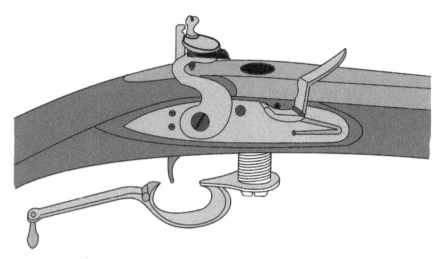

Fig 59: Isaac de la Chaumette@s breech loading system 1704

The system was further improved by Patrick Ferguson. He was familiar with the arm and knew that its biggest problem were the difficulties caused by fouling. He designed a plug that presented a smooth surface to the end of the bore when the breech was closed. He also cut channels in the threads to further reduce fouling and he provided a small space at the back of the plug where smoke and residue could collect. His final improvement was to thicken the bottom of the barrel so that the plug could be dropped entirely below the bore for loading, making access for cleaning much easier.

Ferguson demonstrated his rifle for the Master General of Ordnance at Woolwich in quite unhelpful weather conditions. The day of the demonstration was both very wet and windy. It is unlikely that an ordinary flintlock would have functioned at all on such a day, but Ferguson's rifle performed well. Everyone was impressed and a number of rifles were ordered but British Ordnance wanted a gun that would fire the standard paper cartridge rather than the loose powder and ball that the Ferguson fired. Thus, Ordnance commissioned Durs-Egg, a well-known London gunsmith, to make a number of short carbines with a tip-up breech Fig 60.

A spring clip allowed the rear portion of barrel to tip up so that a cartridge could be inserted. The Austrians had tried such a gun invented by Giuseppe Crespi of Milan in the 1770s but had abandoned it because of problems with leaking gases. The British encountered similar problems and the project was effectively abandoned by the British as well.

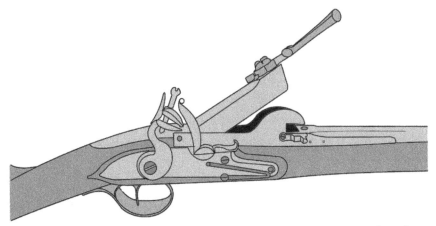

Fig 60: Durrs-Egg breech loading system based on the Crepi tip-up breech

It was left to the Americans to adopt a breech loader as a standard military weapon and this happened in 1819, and the rifle they chose was the Hall rifle. It would seem that Hall, in his own words, was little aquatinted with rifles and was ignorant of any method of loading at the breech. He therefore approached the problem with fresh eyes and developed a tip-up breech with no knowledge of Crespi or the experiences of the Austrians and British. But Hall was not entirely alone. An Architect called William Thornton was working on a similar device and they got together. They obtained a patent in 1811.

The difference to former attempts was that the whole breech, together with the lock, tipped up to load and it had a simple spring catch to hold it in the closed position. The gun performed well in tests and was adopted as an official arm in 1819, Fig 61.

Fig 61: Hall flintloch breech loader 1819

Production of Hall's rifle began at the Harpers Ferry Armoury, where Hall himself designed the machinery to manufacture the rifle on an assembly line basis with completely interchangeable parts. Such systems had been tried before, but Hall's was the first to produce fully interchangeable arms in America and possibly in the world. In fact, Hall's contributions to arms manufacturing far exceeded his contribution to arms design. The rifle itself had problems. There was a tendency for it to leak gas after it became worn and the spring catch for securing the breech stuck out below the stock and often became entangled in clothing or equipment. Nevertheless, it was used successfully, and a percussion carbine soon followed. Soldiers soon discovered with the percussion model, that they could remove the breech block intact and carry it as a pistol.

Hall's rifle was the first breech loader to be adopted as an official arm, but tests and experiments were being carried out all over Europe, where our story now continues.

The possibility of using fulminates in a cartridge that could be detonated without the use of external priming, was first recognised in the early nineteenth century by Samuel Johannes Pauly, a Swiss inventor who travelled to both France and England during the Napoleonic wars.

In 1812 Pauly introduced a radically different double-barrelled fowling piece of breech loading design Fig 62. This arm used a cartridge closely resembling a modern centre-fire cartridge. The charge was ignited by means of a detonating pellet placed in the centre of the brass disc which formed the base. The cartridge was not completely gas-tight however, relying on a felt wad that was attached to the base of the cartridge and entered the barrel when loaded.

The actual cartridge case that contained the charge was made of paper and was completely consumed on firing. The brass base and felt wad were extracted after firing and could be used again with a new cartridge case.

Despite their success for use in sporting guns the new cartridges were considered too difficult to manufacture and therefore too expensive for military use.

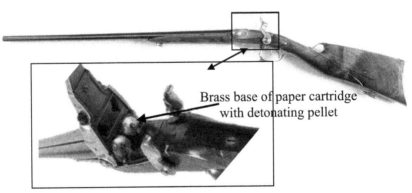

Brass base of paper cartridge with detonating pellet

Fig 62: Pauly's breech loader

Around 1838 Johann Nikolaus von Dreyse produced a breech loading rifle which used a lead bullet with a percussion compound in a hollow at its base. It was detonated by a long needle that passed through the powder charge and struck the priming compound. It was a self-contained round in just the same way as a modern cartridge, and the breech loading system that he employed was in all essentials the bolt action we see in the twentieth century Fig 63.

Fig 63: Dreyse breech loading rifle

The main disadvantages of the Dreyse system was that the long firing pin had a tendency to bend or break easily, possibly aggravated by being in the middle of the burning charge each time the gun was fired. In 1866 Antoine Alphonse Chassepot improved Dreyse's bolt action by using a shorter firing pin which struck an inverted percussion cap in the head of the cartridge.

The last of the important breech loaders were the Sharps rifle and carbine. Christian Sharps was granted a patent in 1848. With this gun, a breechblock slid vertically in a mortice cut in the receiver.

The trigger guard acted as a lever and when this was pulled down the block was lowered, exposing the chamber so that the cartridge could be inserted. When the trigger guard was returned to its normal position the breechblock was raised and a blade cut open the base of the cartridge exposing the powder within to the flame from the primer.

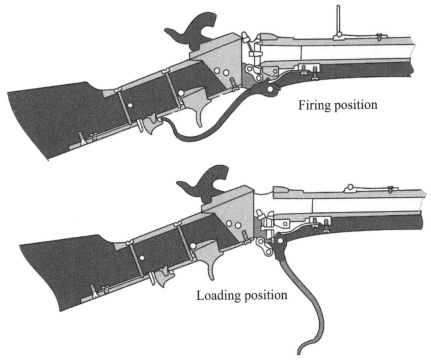

Firing position

Loading position

Fig 64: Sharps drop breech-block

Fig 65: Sharps carbine

Sharps tried several systems before opting for a disc that was automatically fed over the nipple as the hammer fell. This system proved so successful that it continued to be used for later single-shot rifles, such as Winchester, Stevens and Farquharson, which used a self-sealing cartridge.

Fig 66: Later Winchster single shot rifle with a drop breech-block

Sharps rifles were popular with everyone from soldiers to buffalo hunters and marksmen. Special target rifles were produced with precision sights that won acclaim in competitions, and The London Sporting Gazette described the Sharps rifle as "unequalled."

John Brown used Sharps carbines in a raid on the Federal armoury at Harpers Ferry, Virginia in 1859. His intention was to obtain more arms with which to arm slaves and lead them in a rebellion against their owners in the South.

The plot failed, Brown was captured and then hanged at nearby Charlestown. The Sharps models 1852 and 1853 with the slanting breech and brass mounts are known to collectors in America as "John Brown Sharps."

It was also the Sharps regular carbine and the special long-range model that buffalo hunters used and was largely responsible for the decimation of the herds of bison that once roamed the American plains.

In 1878 a new Sharps, designed by Hugo Borchardt was produced and this new gun was very different to the earlier models, and after the American Civil War many were converted to take the new self-contained metallic cartridge that had proved to be so superior to the old paper one.

Apart from the change in ammunition however, the rifle remained almost unaltered.

In late 1877 the Borchardt improvement permitted the introduction of a new hammerless line of rifles with an enclosed firing pin in the breech, but the new weapon never really caught on and the Sharps Rifle Company suspended operations in 1881.

The American Civil War had seen a plethora of different breech loading systems. There were tilting barrels, sliding barrels, sliding, dropping, rotating or tilting breech-blocks as well as bolt-action.

Some were good and some not so good. Few lasted very long, simply because none were as good or performed as well as the Sharps.

Meanwhile, French gunsmiths and inventors such as Pottet, Flobert, Le Faucheux and Houillier had been building on Pauly's idea of a truly self-contained cartridge.

The first success was a cartridge with a percussion cap mounted sideways in its base. A pin, poised above it, projected through the case and gave it its name, "pin-fire." The blow from the hammer when the trigger was squeezed drove the pin into the cap and set off the charge, Fig 67.

The system worked well but the cartridges themselves were vulnerable as the exposed pin could be broken off or struck accidentally, with unfortunate results.

Various other systems were tried. There were teat-fires, with the primer in a little projection at the head of the cartridge; lip-fires with the primer in a protuberance on the rim; enclosed pin-fires, with the pin covered by the casing, and a number of others.

Then in 1858 two Americans, Horace Smith and Daniel Wesson produced a rim-fire cartridge that won quick approval and was used in a variety of firearms. In these cartridges the priming compound was distributed in a ring around the base of the cartridge. When the trigger is squeezed, releasing the hammer, the firing pin crushes the rim igniting the primer.

The problem with rim-fire cartridges however, was that it was difficult to produce a metal, soft enough to be easily indented by the hammer of the gun, but strong enough to withstand the explosion of a heavy charge. The rim-fire was limited for this reason to using weak loads for the main charge.

The centre-fire cartridge removed this shortcoming. Many inventors in England, France and the United States contributed to the development of the centre-fire cartridge, and they were made in England as early as 1852.

The system was perfected by Colonel Hiram Berdan of Civil War sharpshooting fame and by Colonel Edward M. Boxer of the British Royal Laboratory in 1866 and there have been no major changes since.

The American Civil War had shown the superiority of breech loaders and after the war many muzzle loading muskets were converted using a method devised by Erskine S. Allin of the Springfield Armoury.

Conversions began in 1865 and eventually the Allin system became the .45-70 Springfield, adopted as the standard infantry weapon of the US army in 1873.

Nicknamed the "Springfield Trapdoor," the rifle would serve the American military for the next twenty years. The rifle got its nickname from its breech-loading mechanism, which resembled a trapdoor Fig 67. To load a round, a soldier had to open the latch and manually insert a single cartridge.

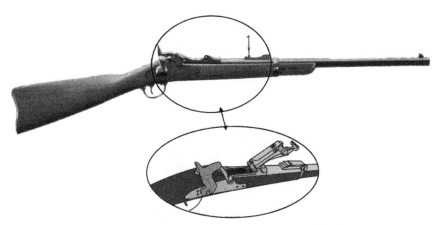

Fig 67: The Springfield "Trap-door" breech loader

Although selected by a board of officers, the Springfield was not universally considered the best weapon. Many American and foreign experts thought that both the Remington and the Peabody were superior.

There were reports that the spent cartridges could be difficult to remove after the gun had been fired several times, and the American Press were quick to seise on this after the disastrous defeat of George Armstrong Custer and five troops of the Seventh Cavalry, by Sitting Bull at the Battle of the Little Big Horn.

Despite this, the Springfield served throughout the Plains Indian Wars and the Spanish-American War, indeed, some state troops were still armed with it at the beginning of American involvement in World War 1.

In Great Britain the change over from muzzle to breech loaders also came about when there were large stocks of muzzle loaders that the government did not want to waste.

In 1865 Britain selected a conversion system designed by Jacob Snider of New York. This was also based on a hinged breech-block, but unlike the Springfield, the Snider breech-block was hinged on the side and swung out to the right of the weapon for loading Fig 68.

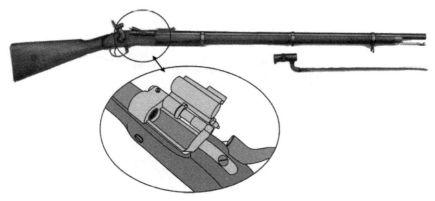

Fig 68: Snider conversion of an Enfield 1867-1869

The Snider conversion also had problems with extraction of the spent cartridge which meant that the gun had to be turned upside-down to eject it. Nevertheless, it proved to be a good weapon.

Unlike the American Springfield however the Snider-Enfield was only ever intended as a stop-gap, and a board of officers was convened to make a study of all the available breech-loading systems. In the end they looked at one hundred and twenty different actions and forty-nine different cartridges.

The eventual decision was to go for the breech loading system known as the Peabody-Martini. Peabody had patented a system known as the falling block in 1862. In this system, the block was pivoted at the back and pulling on a lever, usually the trigger guard, tilted the block forward at the front exposing the chamber. Fig 69 shows the original Peabody rifle.

Fig 69: The Peabody rifle

In Switzerland the Peabody came to the attention of one Frederich von Martini. Martini did away with the traditional hammer system that Peabody had used, and introduced an internal self-cocking striker. This increased the speed of action and gave it protection, producing a very fine gun that was adopted by the British in 1871.

The new gun was coupled with a barrel designed by Alexander Henry of Edinburgh and, I'm sure much to the dismay of Peabody, became known as the Martini-Henry Fig 70.

The Martini-Henry was the back-bone of the British army and saw service with a variety of different barrels in Burma, Malaya, India, South Africa, South America, West Indies and Afghanistan.

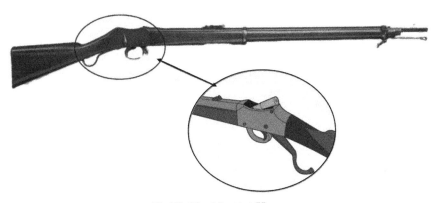

Fig 70: The Martini-Henry

There was another, extremely good, breech loading system developed at the close of the American Civil War and that was the Remington rolling block. Leonard Geiger and Joseph Rider developed the system at the Remington plant in 1865, just as General Lee was surrendering to Ulysses S. Grant.

The rolling block operated by cocking the hammer and then pulling or rolling the breech-block back with the thumb. The cartridge was inserted and the block pushed back into position, while a locking lever held the hammer cocked and locked the breech closed. When the trigger was pulled, the hammer struck a firing pin mounted in the breech-block and added its weight to the breech at the moment of discharge. The system was so cleverly designed that the pressure of the explosion forced the parts more tightly together, meaning that the greater the recoil the tighter the seal Fig 71.

At the proving house at Liege in Belgium a .50 calibre Remington was loaded with 750 grains of black powder, 40 balls and two wads so that the barrel was completely full, a charge over thirty inches long. After firing, the director of proof noted that "nothing extraordinary occurred."

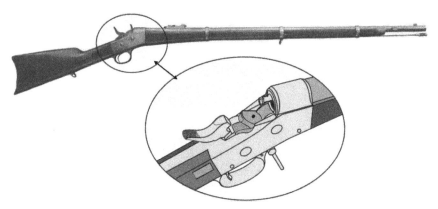

Fig 71: The Reminton rolling-block

By 1870, all of the principal breech loaders had been invented. The bolt action, trap door, falling block, rolling block, drop block and the tip-down barrel were all widely used, with the Remington being possibly the best of the lot.

The age of the muzzle loader was over, but ironically, the single shot breech loader was now also obsolete. The invention and perfecting of the self-contained metal cased cartridge had issued in the age of the repeater. Who would want to load after every shot, when he could own a gun with its own fully stocked magazine?

Chapter 7

To Load Once but
Fire Often

Everybody misses, even marksmen occasionally, but having to reload and take the shot again can be more than just an embarrassment, especially if your target is shooting back. The ability to fire more than one shot before having to reload had always been a priority for the inventor and gunsmith. Pistols were often made in pairs for just that reason and many pirates of the 17th and 18th centuries would carry more than one pair, indeed, there are reports of some carrying as many as eight pistols about their person.

Interestingly, most types of multiple shot weapon had been thought of and tried before 1700 and these included multiple-barrels, revolving cylinders and magazines. The basic ideas came early, refinement took centuries.

We saw earlier in Fig 6, an illustration of a Ribauldequin, and just like it, most of the early multiple-barrel weapons were volley guns, firing all their barrels at the same time, like the famous seven-barrelled example by Nock, shown in Fig 72, or the ducks-foot pistol where the side-by-side barrels are spread out at the front, as previously shown in Fig 28.

Fig 72: Seven barrelled volley gun by Nock 1798

The inventor of the seven-barrelled volley gun shown here was actually James Wilson and he presented his new gun to the board of ordnance for trial in July 1779.

The board was suitably impressed but felt that the weapon would be more useful on-board a ship rather than in the field, so they referred it to the Admiralty.

Nock was commissioned by the Admiralty to make samples, at first with rifled barrels, and orders began to be placed with him, although the rifling was abandoned in favour of a smooth-bore due to the extra cost, the rifled version being £15 each as opposed to £13 each for the smoothbore.

In operation, the flash from the pan ignited the charge in the central chamber, and six small channels or vents, communicated this to the outer barrels, thus the centre barrel fired first, followed quickly by the outer six. The major problem with the gun seems to have been that, if the channels from the central chamber became fouled or clogged up, then a misfire could occur in one or more barrels without the shooter realising.

Over the next few years Nock is reputed to have made over five hundred guns for the Navy and the gun continued to be popular even after the Navy stopped using them. A percussion version was displayed at the Great Exhibition of 1851 and Henry Pieper developed one that fired a .22 rim-fire cartridge with a Remington rolling-block breech.

As for the ducks-foot pistol, it also, surprisingly, proved to be a popular weapon, especially with prison wardens and anyone who was likely to be confronted by an angry mob. When fired into a crowd there was a good chance of hitting someone, and being confronted with it must have had a sobering effect on those at the front.

Many multiple-barrelled guns however were two, three or four barrelled examples that could fire the barrels independently of one another, and there were various methods of achieving that. Some had rotating barrels and some, as was the case with flintlocks, had valves which directed the flash from the pan to the selected barrel.

Sharps patented a four-barrelled pistol in 1859, in which the firing pin rotated each time the gun was cocked Fig 73.

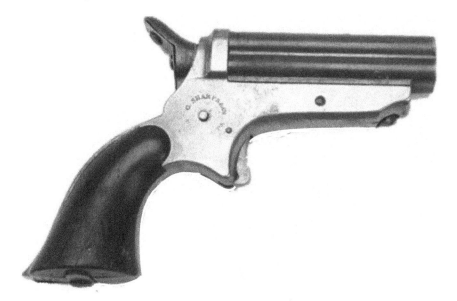

Fig 73: Sharps 1859 patent four barrelled pistol
National Firearms Museum

A similar, although larger, four barrelled gun, was the Lancaster large frame holster pistol shown in Fig 74. Again, a single trigger operates a rotating firing pin and the barrels are hinged for loading. A side lever operated a barrel lock on the top of the frame.

It could be thought of as a modern four barrelled pepper-box pistol popular in the early-mid 19th century. Unlike these earlier guns which had percussion cap ignition, the Lancaster was chambered for the more modern brass cartridges, and could take a .410 shotgun cartridge. It had a faster rate of fire than the standard-issue Adams revolver and was often fitted with a Tranter-type double trigger to overcome the heavy pull required to fire the gun.

The Lancaster pistol enjoyed popularity with British officers in India and Africa during the British Raj owing to its faster rate of fire and increased reliability over contemporary revolvers. It was highly prized by hunters and explorers for close range defence against big game, and unlike revolvers, there is no gap between the chamber and the barrel, so there is no leakage of gas when fired.

Fig 74: Lancaster four barrelled pistol 1881-1890 show both closed and open for loading

Another popular design was the three-barrelled pocket pistol such as the one patented in 1857 by William W. Marston of New York Fig 75. The idea was to have a gun that would lie flat in the pocket. The firing pin moved up after each shot and a circular dial on the outside indicated how many shots had been fired.

Fig 75: Marston thee barrelled pistol 1857
Collectors Firearms

Another example of multiple barrels, this time mounted horizontally, is the so-called harmonica pistol patented by A. E. and P. H. Jarre of Paris in 1873 and shown here in Fig 76.

Fig 76: Harmonica pistol 1873
National Firearms Museum

For carrying, the handle could be moved to the end of the block and twisted so that it was in line with the block rather than at right angles to it.

The double-barrelled derringer was another very popular pocket pistol. Named after Henry Derringer who made the first one, the term "derringer" has come to mean any small pocket pistol that is neither a revolver nor semi-automatic.

Possibly the biggest seller of this type of gun was the Remington double barrelled pistol shown in Fig 77. Its .41-calibre bullets had good stopping power, but with barrels only three inches long, it could easily be concealed in a gentleman's pocket or about a lady's attire. No cowboy film of the forties or fifties would have been complete, unless the heroine defended herself by producing a derringer from her stocking-top.

Fig 77: Remington double-barrelled derringer 1880-1900
National Firearms Museum

The pistol was so popular with the ladies, that during the time of its manufacture from 1866 to 1935, many were produced with fancy pearl grips and engraved plated barrels.

Adding extra barrels was an obvious way of increasing firepower and there are any number of side-by-side, over-and-under and turn-over examples surviving to this day and giving testimony to the ingenuity of the gunsmith. Fig 78, shows a percussion turn-over pistol and a flintlock over and under pistol. The screw on the side of the flintlock is used to redirect the flame between the top and bottom chambers. Side by side four barrelled versions of both types were common.

Turn-over pistol

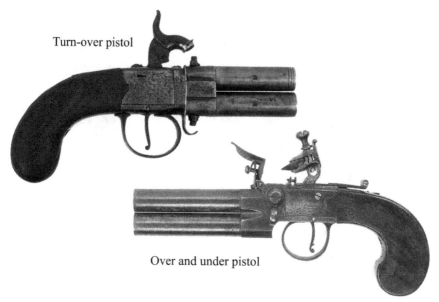

Over and under pistol

Fig : Percussion turn-over and flintlock over and under pistols

Another, if somewhat improbable way of increasing fire-power was the concept of superimposed loads, where a number of charges were loaded in the same barrel, one on top of the other.

In one system the bullets were pierced from front to back and the hole filled with fuse compound. A number of charges, separated by these bullets would then be loaded in the barrel and the foremost one discharged by some means.

If the bullets fitted the bore tightly and the holes in the bullets were properly aligned, the flash from the first charge would ignite the fuse in the hole of the bullet immediately behind it. This fuse would then burn through and ignite the second charge and so on, rather like a Roman Candle firework.

One refinement that was quickly added was the addition of a second lock so that once the initial, superimposed load was exhausted the gun could be loaded and fired as a normal single shot weapon. This was an important refinement because superimposed loads took a great deal of time to load and time was not something you had much of in a battle.

Although many were made and used, the Roman Candle type of superimposed load weapon fell from grace, partly because it was so difficult to load correctly, but also because once set in action it could not be stopped until the gun was empty. The gun of a soldier shot dead or wounded after pulling the trigger was a considerable hazard to his compatriots nearby.

The simple solution seemed to be a sliding lock, and several people made them including John Aitken in England in 1780. In America, Isaiah Jennings patented a rifle with a sliding lock in 1821 and Jacob Mould patented a similar gun in England in 1825, Shown in Fig 78 is a percussion superimposed load pistol with a sliding lock pistol by W. Mills.

Fig 78: percussion superimposed load pistol with a sliding lock pistol by W. Mills.
Royal Armouries Collection

It was the self-contained metal rim-fire or centre-fire cartridge that put an end to this particular line of endeavour. Now there were better ways to ensure one could fire several times before having to re-load.

The Revolving Cylinder

Chapter 8

The Revolving Cylinder

The revolving cylinder goes right back to the time of flint weapons and even before that. Fig 79 shows a snaphaunce revolver of the late seventeenth century, but early examples such as this are very rare, as the revolver did not really become practical until the appearance of the percussion cap in the early ninetieth century, greatly simplified the revolver's mechanism and reduced the number of motions necessary for firing a succession of shots.

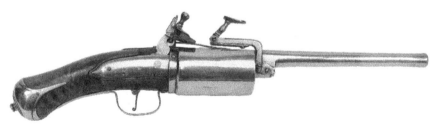

Fig 79: Six shot snaphaunce revolver 1660-1670
The Royal Armouries Collection

A major problem with the design of any revolver is obtaining a good seal and alignment between the chambers and the barrel. The first man to try and market a revolver on any sort of a large scale was James Puckle. He produced a large revolving cylinder gun that stood on a tripod. Puckle described it as "a portable gun or machine called a defence, yet discharges so often and so many bullets and can be so quickly loaded as renders it next to impossible to carry any ship by boarding."

Puckle's weapon, that he patented in 1718, consisted of tripod mounted frame and barrel that could be loaded with pre-loaded cylinders that were revolved by hand. The chambers each had a coned face that fitted into the countersunk breech and there was a crank at the back, by which the cylinder could be screwed up tight against the barrel for each shot. This ensured that the chamber to be fired was correctly aligned and had an effective gas-tight seal, Fig 80.

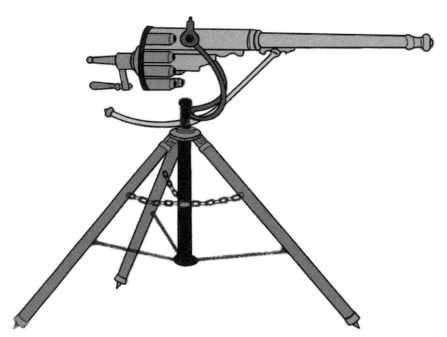

Fig 80: A drawing of James Puckle's gun

A feature of the gun was its adaptability. It could be fired by match or flint and Puckle declared that it could fire round bullets against Christians or square bullets, that were thought to be more effective against infidels. Special cylinders were provided for either contingency.

Puckle went to great lengths to advertise and market his gun but all to no avail, despite the fact that after one demonstration in 1722, the London Journal reported that a Puckle gun was fired sixty-three times in seven minutes during a rainstorm.

Succeeding years of the eighteenth century saw other flintlock revolvers produced throughout England and Europe. Some were muskets and some handguns but all had their problems.

The first practical flintlock revolver may have been invented by Captain Artemus Wheeler of Concord Massachusetts, who obtained a patent for "a gun to discharge seven or more times" on June 10th 1818, almost one hundred years after Puckle. Wheeler tried to interest the Navy but failed, and obviously disheartened, he gave up manufacturing the gun.

Shortly after the patent was granted, Elisha Collier of Boston sailed for England and obtained an English patent, while Cornelious Coolridge, also of Boston, travelled to France and obtained a patent there. Whether Collier and Coolridge were working for Wheeler or not is unknown, but it seems unlikely. When taking out his English patent Collier made no claim to complete originality and his patent did include some improvements to the Wheeler design. Collier's pistol included a priming magazine and an improved joint between barrel and chamber. In fact, Collier reversed Puckle's design and had a coned breech and countersunk chambers.

In the case of the Collier revolver, shown in Fig 81, it was necessary, after firing a shot, to cock the lock, rotate the cylinder by hand and then close the cover of the flash-pan over the primer. The frizzen was mounted on the right of the barrel, as would be found on a standard flintlock pistol. The rotation of the cylinder permits the touch-hole, which has a sliding cover, to line up with the frizzen. In percussion hand-rotated guns, these actions were reduced to two, cocking the pistol and rotating the cylinder.

It is surprising that, although many Collier flintlock revolvers were later converted to percussion, Collier himself appears to have stopped making revolving pistols when the percussion era came in and returned to civil engineering.

Fig 81: Collier flintlock revolver c1800.
Ian McCullum Forgotten Weapons

The pistol that replaced the Collier was the percussion pepper-box revolver.

The Pepperbox

The first pepper-box revolvers had cylinders that had to be rotated by hand after each shot, Fig 82, but sometime towards the end or soon after the 1830s, self cocking models can be found that also incorporate the automatic rotation of the barrels, the action of which is shown in Fig 83.

Fig 82: Hand rotated pepper-box with folding trigger 1830
Collectors Firearms

With these pistols, pressure on the trigger caused the hammer to rise and fall, a movement known as double action because the trigger effectively both cocks and fires the pistol.

Pepper-box revolver

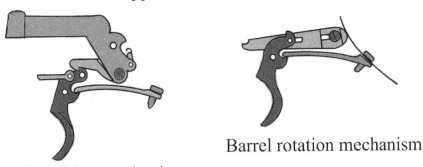

Barrel rotation mechanism

Self-cocking mechanism

Fig 83: Self cocking and rotation mechanisms for the pepper-box

Although these pistols had the advantage of being able to fire five or six shots rapidly, the amount of pressure needed on the trigger and the fact that the hammer resided on the top of the gun prevented accurate aiming. Nevertheless, they became very popular both in Europe and in America, Fig 84.

Fig 84: A double action self-rotating Pepperbox revolver 1845

One unusual form of hand-rotated pepper-box was the Budding revolver. Edwin Budding is best remembered as the inventor of the first mechanical lawn-mower. His pistol differs considerably from other pepper-box types in having completely enclosed nipples set in line with the axis of the barrels. The hammer slides horizontally in line with the nipple of the lowest barrel and is operated by a spiral spring ,Fig 85.

In order to cock the gun, the hammer is drawn back for a distance of about one inch and moved slightly to the right where it engages in a small notch in the side of the slot. There is no separate trigger, so to fire, the shooter must press the hammer to the left with the tip of his fore-finger, releasing it from the notch and allowing it to spring forward striking the nipple.

In order to re-load, the cylinder must be removed by un-screwing the steel pin on which it revolves, as this is the only way to access the spent percussion caps. The steel pin is used as a ramrod for charging the cylinders.

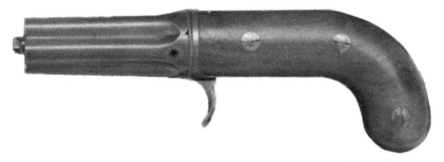

Fig 85: A Budding's pepper-box pistol.

Apart from Budding's pistol, English pepperbox revolvers differed little, other than in size and quality of manufacture. The only real exception was the Cooper pepper-box introduced into England in the early 1840s. Based on French and Belgium revolvers of the Mariette system, that was patented in Belgium in1837. The main difference with the Cooper system was the arrangement of the nipples.

On the more common pepper-box, the nipples are sighted at right angles to the axis of the barrels, whereas the Cooper model has them in line and separated from each other by partitions. The hammer also differed from the normal gun in being partially enclosed in the body of the pistol and striking the bottom rather than the top nipple Fig 86.

Fig 86: The Cooper model pepper-box

The advantages of this arrangement were twofold. The partitions between the nipples greatly reduce the chance of accidental discharge and the re-sighting of the hammer underneath the pistol meant that it was possible to take aim along the top barrel.

Transition revolvers

Throughout the later years of the pepperbox era, many attempts were made to improve its range and accuracy by devising a long-barrelled arm with a mechanically rotating cylinder.

It was Samuel Colt in America who patented such a weapon in 1836. This was the first rifled revolving pistol to combine the actions of cocking and of rotating the cylinder in a single motion. Colt's pistol was a single action, that is to say the gun could only be discharged after it had been manually cocked.

The cylinder, rotated by being connected to the hammer by a pawl, featured horizontal nipples, separated from each other by partitions. The pawl acted upon a toothed ratchet wheel attached to the base of the cylinder. Colt produced these guns between 1836 and 1842 and they were widely used in America but were not introduced into Europe in any numbers until after 1850.

Colt's patent seriously affected the design of English revolvers between 1840 and 1850 by preventing the use of horizontally arranged nipples and of the ratchet and pawl mechanism of the type used by Colt.

His patent therefore limited English gun makers to adapting the pepper-box mechanism that had been in use before Colt's patent. English revolvers of the eighteen forties therefore consisted of the standard pepper-box for the pocket, and a transition type revolver, that combined the self-cocking mechanism of the pepper-box with the use of a single fixed barrel and a six-chamber revolving cylinder of reduced length.

This transition type of gun forms a link between the fairly crude pepper-box and the modern revolver.

The transition revolver still possessed the difficulties of aiming due to the position of the hammer and the excessively heavy trigger-pull caused by the self-cocking mechanism and in addition, there was now an even more serious shortcoming. The barrel on the early guns was simply screwed to the cylinder pin without any additional support. There was a tendency for the barrel to became loose with continued use and that was extremely undesirable, Fig 87.

Fig 87: Early transition revolver

The solution was to add a strap connecting the body of the gun to the breech end of the barrel as shown in Fig 88.

Fig 88: Later transition revolver with sopport strap

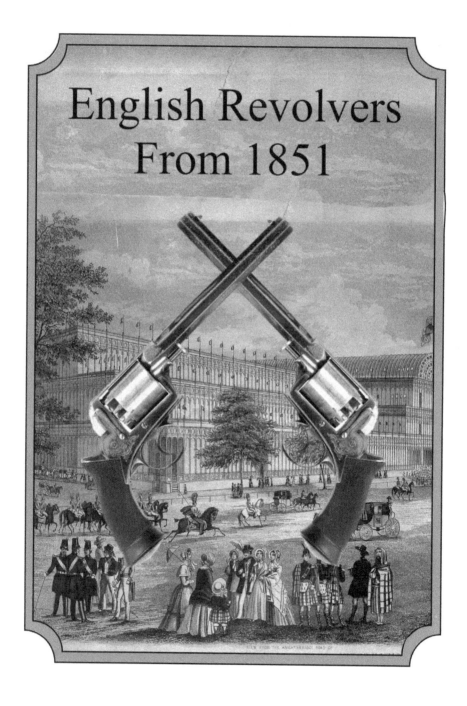

English Revolvers
From 1851

Chapter 9

English Revolvers from 1851

It can be understood from the previous chapter on transition revolvers, that no exploration of English pistols at that time can go by without a mention of Samuel Colt and an examination of his guns. He greatly influenced the design and development of revolvers worldwide.

It was at the Great Exhibition of 1851 that Colt introduced his revolver to the wider world. It was not a new invention because Colt had been producing the gun at his factories in Paterson, New Jersey and later at Hartford, Connecticut, since 1836 when he took out his patent.

Colt came to England, not just to exhibit his guns at the Great Exhibition but also to look for a suitable site for a European factory. At the Exhibition, his gun met with almost universal acclaim, not because of the mechanism itself, which was possibly open to some criticism, but because of the robust character of the weapon and the method of manufacture.

Colt sought to do away with hand-work wherever possible and brought in a system of working with templates, patterns and gauges. This was to ensure that all the parts of a particular model would be completely interchangeable and if a part had to be replaced it could be done with very little filing and adjustment.

Colt gave a lecture on his improved mass-production methods to the Institute of Civil Engineering in 1851. A lecture for which he received the "Telford" gold medal.

The London factory operated between 1853 and 1857 and was run on the same lines as his American operations. The bulk of his staff, recruited in London, were unskilled or semi-skilled workers but the foremen and key workers were men trained at his factory in Hartford.

Colt's factory was basically independent of the established gun trade and it was capable of turning out extremely reliable arms at a price that made competition difficult. This was not easy for the established trade to accept and there followed a great deal of criticism and abuse. There were accusations of shoddy workmanship and sharp practices at the factory and personal attacks upon Colt himself.

Any real examination of the guns produced at the factory at that time however, would have given the lie to the claims, and in fact, no lesser person than Charles Dickens, who visited the factory in 1854, and was fully aware of the sort of conditions that existed in such places, declared himself to have been most favourably impressed by the smooth and efficient working of the whole system, the neat finish of the arms and the excellent working conditions and high wages of the operatives. Dickens also states that the output of the factory was 600 finished arms per week and at the time of his visit, the storeroom was empty because demand was obviously far outstripping supply.

The London factory was producing four different models: the Navy Revolver (Fig 64), a six-chamber weapon of .360 calibre with a seven-inch barrel, and a range of five chamber .310 calibre pocket and belt pistols with barrel lengths of four, five and six inches. Both the Navy and pocket models were of similar design having a fixed trigger with guard and a rammer or plunger shaped to fit the conical Colt bullet and operated by a lever hinged below the barrel.

Fig 89: Navy Colt 1851
National Firearms Museum

The revolving mechanism consisted of a lever or pawl that was attached to the hammer and operated upon a toothed ratchet cut on the base of the cylinder, causing it to rotate as the hammer was moved to full cock. A spring attached to the pawl, pressed against the frame of the pistol, keeping it in close contact with the cylinder during cocking A in Fig 90.

Another part of Colt's mechanism was the cylinder-bolt or stop that secured the cylinder in the firing position B in Fig 90. The cylinder-bolt was fixed see-saw fashion upon a screw passing through the gun frame. The front end was shaped to fit into a corresponding series of slots cut into the surface of the cylinder and was held in place by a light spring.

As the hammer was raised, it lifted the back end of the cylinder-bolt, depressing the front and allowing the cylinder to revolve freely until the hammer reached full-cock, when the bolt was released and snapped back into position, once again locking the cylinder in place. When the trigger was pulled and the hammer fell, the hind part of the cylinder bolt, which was made of spring steel, was pressed slightly to the side allowing the hammer to pass, after which it sprung back into place ready for the next shot.

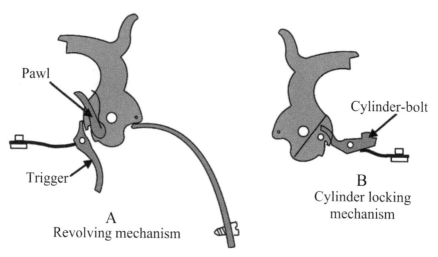

Pawl

Cylinder-bolt

Trigger

B
Cylinder locking
mechanism

A
Revolving mechanism

Fig 90: Colt's revolving mechanism

The list price for a standard Navy Colt, together with bullet-mould casting both round and conical bullets, a cleaning rod and a combined turn-screw and nipple-key was £5–10–0. The price of the pocket revolver was £4-0–0 with the same accessories. Plain wooden boxes or holsters could be purchased as extras and prices could be supplied for specially engraved presentation pieces in mahogany or rosewood cases.

The price list also contained prices for the much larger, six chambered .44 calibre Dragoon revolver that was fitted with a seven-and-a-half-inch barrel. Although examples of the Dragoon revolver are found with the London address on them, there is no evidence that they were ever manufacture at the London factory. The Dragoon revolvers have the London address engraved on them, whereas the Navy and pocket pistols actually made at the London plant, have the address stamped on.

It is known that some Navy and pocket pistols were shipped to London from Hartford for sale before the London base was in production and these pistols have the address engraved on them, so it seems likely that the Dragoon pistols sold from London, were in fact manufactured in America.

It mustn't be assumed that because Colt's revolver was such a success at the 1851 exhibition and had impressive sales figures that it had no rivals. The Lang revolver was the final word in transition type pistols and also sold well.

The Lang revolver was a six chambered, single action pistol that had the barrel end of the chambers countersunk to accept the cone shaped end of the barrel. Barrel and cylinder were kept in close contact by a steel wedge that was thrust forward by the fall of the hammer creating a gas tight seal. The hammer, which had a long thumb piece, was fitted slightly to the right of the central axis of the gun in order to give a clear line of sight for aiming, Fig 91. The barrel was rifled and was attached to the pistol by means of a cross-bolt passing through a slot in the cylinder-pin.

Fig 91: A Lang revolver c1855.

In its early form, made in the late 1840s, the Lang revolver had vertical nipples with no partition between them and no mechanical rammer. The pistol shown in Fig 91 is from 1855 and is fitted with a rammer.

The Lang pattern revolver appears to have been made by a number of different London gunsmiths between 1851 and 1860.

There were other variations of the Lang revolver, notably the Witton and Daw pistol, that differed from the Lang model by having partitions between the nipples and a loading rammer of the Colt type, improvements that were made possible by the expiration of the Colt patent in 1851.

There were of course, other rivals to Colt such as the Parker-field revolver and the Baker revolver, show in Fig 92.

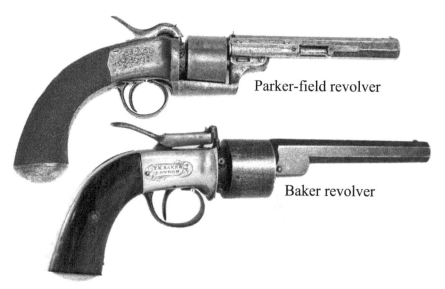

Fig 92: The Parker-field revolver and Baker revolver.

Possibly the most formidable rival to Colt however, was the Deane-Adams revolver shown in Fig 93.

Fig 93: Deane Adams double action revolver with a spurless hammer 1851

A five-chamber double action pistol, (double action because pulling the trigger, both cocked and fired the gun), it differed from both the Lang and Colt revolvers in being of solid frame construction, that is to say one in which both the barrel and the frame of the pistol were shaped in a single forging.

The cylinder had horizontal nipples separated by partitions and was pivoted on a moveable pin that was held in position by a spring catch and could be removed for cleaning.

The revolving and self-cocking mechanisms of the Deane-Adams revolver are shown in Fig 94.

They consist of a pawl acting on a toothed ratchet at the base of the cylinder and a "lifter" that engaged in a notch at the front of the hammer that are both linked to the back of the trigger.

When the trigger was pulled, the hammer was raised by the lifter until it reached a point where pressure from the front of the hammer against the back of the lifter forced its point clear of the notch in the hammer, allowing it to fall.

Simultaneously with the cocking of the pistol, the five-chambered cylinder was rotated by the action of the pawl until the uppermost chamber was in line with the barrel. At this point the partition separating the two lowest chambers come into contact with a stop which formed part of the trigger and which rose through an aperture in the frame of the gun as the trigger was drawn back, locking the cylinder in place.

Once the gun was discharged and the trigger released a V-spring returned it to the firing position ready for the next shot, Fig 94.

Self-cocking action of the
Deane-Adams revolver

Revolving mechanism of the
Deane-Adams revolver

Fig 94:

The Deane-Adams revolver was made in three standard models roughly corresponding the Dragoon, Navy and pocket models of the Colt company.

Although the parts of the Deane-Adams were not as inter-changeable as the Colt models, it was a mass-produced weapon and was manufactured in large quantities at the Deane-Adams factory in Southwark, as well as by various contractors in Birmingham and Liege.

As might be expected there was great rivalry between Colt and Adams and it was bitter rivalry rather than friendly. Sup-porters of Colt were adamant that a double-action or "self-cocking" revolver was totally unsound and could have no value, an opinion that was surely based on the self-cocking pepper-box and transition revolvers that preceded the Adams.

In truth both makes had their advantages and disadvantages. Colt had an advantage in range and accuracy which made it a better weapon in skirmishes, whilst the Adams revolver was better suited to close hand-to-hand fighting in which hard hitting and quick shooting was of more value.

As far as the actual design was concerned, apart from the question of whether single or double action was preferred, the Adams had a one-piece frame that made it stronger and more durable than the Colt system of having a separate barrel. The hammer on the Adams also struck the nipples through an aperture in the frame, making it almost impossible for fragments of spent percussion cap to make their way past the hammer and penetrate into the lock. A minor accident that caused occasional miss-fires in the Colt pistol.

On the other hand, the Colt had the advantage of being fitted with an efficient mechanical rammer that seated a conical bullet with its axis precisely lined with the barrel, and made it possible for the pistol to be loaded with a ball that had a slightly larger bore than the chamber.

The last point is an important one because that method of loading ensured a damp proof seal, as well as eliminating the chance of one discharge escaping through the small gap between the barrel and the front of the chamber and setting off charges in the others, a form of accident that transition revolvers were particularly prone to, and from which the Adams revolver was not immune.

The rivalry between Adams and Colt and their struggle to promote their guns as the better arm, took on more importance when the British War Office began to recognise the importance of the revolver as a military arm.

During the Spring of 1854 a committee, appointed by the War Office, tested both the Colt and the Adams pistols at Woolwich. Although the tests were not conclusive, the Board of Ordnance, without officially adopting it as a service arm,

purchased as many as 40,000 pistols of the Navy model between 1854 and 1856. The guns supplied to the British Government can be identified by their being stamped with "W.D."
together with the broad arrow of the War Department and "T.
P." which denotes the Tower Proof House.

Despite the large order it would seem that the higher military authorities were still unconvinced of the revolvers value
as a military weapon. Even though Britain was engaged in
a Continental war at the time of purchase, no new weapons
were issued to troops bound for the Crimea, and only a small
number were supplied to the Navy for the use of officers. Evan
at the time of the Indian Mutiny when thousands of revolvers
were in store, only a few were issued. Officers on the front
line however, unlike their superiors, appreciated the revolvers
value, and in both the Crimean and Indian campaigns the revolver was in general use with officers purchasing their own.

It is interesting to note that in the Crimea the favoured
weapon was the Colt, but during the Indian campaign, just
three years later, it was the Adams that was the favoured
pistol. A circumstance due in part to the experience gained
in actual warfare, and in part to improvements made to the
Adams pistol between 1854 and 1857.

The case for the Adams revolver was highlighted by two
reported incidents, first from the Crimea when J. G. Crosse of
the 88th Regiment wrote the following to Adams:

*"I had one of the largest-sized revolver pistols at the bloody
battle of Inkermann and by some chance got surrounded by Rus-
sians. I then found the advantages of your pistol over that of
Colonel Colt's, for had I to cock before each shot I should have
lost my life. I should not have had time to cock, as they were
too close to me, being only a few yards from me; so close that
I was bayonetted through the thigh immediately after shooting
the forth man."*

Speaking of the Sepoy Mutiny in India, Lieutenant Colonel G. V. Fosbury reported:

"An officer, who especially prided himself on his pistol shooting, was attacked by a stalwart mutineer armed with a heavy sword. The officer, unfortunately for himself, carried a Colt's Navy pistol, which, as you may remember, was of small calibre, .36, and fired a sharp-pointed picket bullet of sixty to the pound and a heavy charge of powder, its range being at least 600 yards, as I have frequently proved. This he proceeded to empty into the sepoy as he advanced, but having done so, he waited just one second too long to see the effect of his shooting and was cloven to the teeth by his antagonist, who then dropped down and died beside him. My informant, who witnessed the affair, told me that five out of the six bullets had struck the sepoy close together in the chest and had all passed through him and out at his back."

Those reports show two of the types of experiences gained in combat. The most important improvement to the Adams revolver was undoubtedly the introduction of the Beaumont double action patented in February 1855 and shown in Fig 95.

The Beaumont mechanism allowed the gun to be fired, either from the full cock position or with the self-cocking motion, whichever was desired at the time. This was achieved with the addition of a small sear, fitted with a sear-spring, that engaged in a full-cock notch cut in the upper part of the hammer. If the hammer was drawn back by the thumb it would be retained in the full-cock position by the sear. From that position, slight pressure on the trigger would cause the lifter to press against the underside of the sear, lifting it clear of the notch and so releasing the hammer. If on the other hand, the trigger was pulled first, without cocking the hammer, the hammer would be first raised and then released by the action of the lifter as in the original Adams pistol, whilst the fact that the release of the hammer would coincide with the act of the lifter striking on and lifting the sear, would prevent the sear from engaging in the notch in the hammer.

Fig 95: The Beaumont double action patent 1855

With the introduction of the Beaumont double action some other minor changes were made to the outward appearance of the pistol. The butt being less at right-angles to the axis of the pistol and being shaped with a comb to fit above the V of the thumb and forefinger of the shooter, rather like the handle of a carpenter's saw, Fig 96.

The company of Deane, Adams and Deane was dissolved some time in 1856 when the Adams patents were taken over by The London Armoury Company in which Adams features as a co-director with Mr. John Kerr.

Fig 96: The Beaumont-Adams revolver 1856

The adoption of the Adams as the standard service revolver of the British Army marked the end of the great Adams-Colt controversy of the early fifties and destroyed any hopes that Colt may have had of securing any further large contracts from the British Government.

It cannot be a coincidence that the Organisation of The London Armoury Company for the production of the improved double action Adams revolver coincided with Colt's decision to close down his London factory, even though his Hartford factory had been enlarged and was now capable of producing all of Colt's revolvers.

Although Colt closed his London factory, his revolvers remained popular and they continued to sell well in Britain and in Europe, and despite the fact that the Adams revolver was adopted by the British War Office, it was not without numerous rivals.

The years between 1851 and 1860 were rich in English revolver patents and saw the introduction of revolvers by

Kerr, Harvey, Pennell, Bentley, Westley-Richards, Webley, Daw, Deane-Harding and probably Adams closest rival, Tranter.

Tranter and Webley were the two closest rivals of the Adams revolver with Tranter being hailed as amongst the best made and most accurate of the day. Webley, although less well finished than either the Adams or the Tranter, as well as being a cheaper option, nevertheless had a reputation as a solid dependable weapon and sold in large numbers.

Apart from the trigger, the first Tranter modal closely resembled the Adams double action revolver but incorporated an ingenious double action system that allowed the gun to be fired from full-cock or with a self-cocking action, Fig 98.

The action was achieved by having the lower end of the lifter, which raised the hammer and was pivoted on the rear of the trigger, pass through a slot in the centre of the trigger.

The trigger itself was extended to pass through a slot in the trigger guard and project below it in the form of a second spur-trigger. A second trigger, pivoted on the same screw as the spur-trigger pressed on the lower end of the lifter, Fig 99.

Fig 98: Tranter double action revolver

In using the mechanism, it was necessary to use the first two fingers of the hand to operate the two triggers. Firm pressure applied by the second finger on the spur-trigger brought the hammer to full-cock and a lighter pressure on the upper trigger with the forefinger fired the weapon, whilst pulling both triggers at once would fire the pistol with a rapid self-cocking motion, Fig 99.

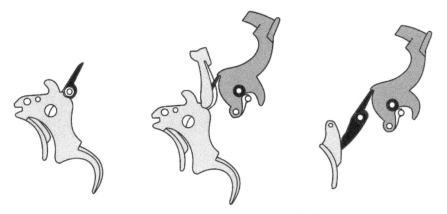

Fig 99: Tranter's double action mechanism

Although this may sound complicated when written down it was found to be very effective in use. The double action gave a rapid rate of fire white the single action gave greater accuracy and the double trigger helped the shooter hold the arm steady and somewhat avoid the tendency of all revolvers to throw a trifle high.

Another feature of the Tranter was the addition of a rammer or loading lever. This was not attached to the pistol at first but carried separately and could be fitted onto a steel peg screwed into the frame of the gun.

The Tranter bullet had to be rammed home with some force because of its snug fit in the chamber, and for this reason had a groove near its base that was filled with a lubricating compound of beeswax and tallow.

On discharge the force of the explosion closed up the groove, forcing out the lubricating compound which mixed with the fouling residue produced by the burning powder to prevent it clogging the grooves of the rifling. Each successive shot effectively cleaned the rifling of the residue from the previous one.

A slightly later model of the Tranter was produced after 1856 with a single trigger. This double-action pistol was made as a pocket gun of .380 calibre with one and a quarter and one and a half inch barrels.

This model also had the rammer that was fixed to the left-hand side of the gun and was secured to the side of the barrel when not in use , Fig 100.

The mechanism of the single trigger Tranter revolver differed from that of the Beaumont-Adams model in that, although it included a lifter and a pawl similar to those in the Adams gun, the sear was positioned immediately behind the trigger and acted upon half-cock and full-cock bents cut in the lower part of the hammer.

Fig 100: Tranter's aingle trigger double action revolver

The sear was released from the full-cock bent by pressure from a spur that projected from the back of the trigger Fig 101. The spur at the back of the trigger was not only used in Tranter models of the sixties and seventies but was widely copied by other manufacturers.

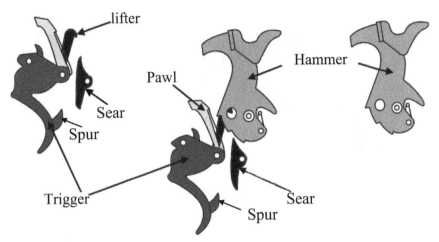

Fig 101: Double action single trigger mechanisum

Both the double trigger and single trigger Tranters were popular and both were sold in large numbers between 1856 and 1863

As for the Webley pistols of the same period, it is more difficult to trace them because they were only marked with the names of the retailers, making it difficult to distinguish them from guns supplied by other manufacturers to the retail trade.

One weapon produced by Webley at that time was a single-action gun known as the Longspur, so called because of the unusually long thumb piece on the hammer, shown in Fig 102.

The barrel was forged separately to the body and was attached by means of either a hinge and a cross-bolt passing through the end of the cylinder pin, or by being screwed onto the end of the cylinder pin and secured with a thumb-screw.

These single-action guns differed from the majority of the Webley pistols by being well finished and engraved, some being marked "Webley's Patent," on the lock.

The double-action Webley on the other hand was plain and was obviously produced in large numbers to sell at a low price.

Fig 102: Webley Longspur

In outward appearance, apart from the quality of finish, it resembled the single-action, being a five chambered .450 calibre weapon with a separately forged barrel screwed to the cylinder pin and secured with a thumb-screw.

The self-cocking or double-action mechanism was an adaptation of the type common to the earlier pepper-box and transition revolvers, the only real difference being the addition of a spring safety-catch, invented by J. Bentley and fitted on the head of the hammer, which held it clear of the nipples while the pistol was loaded, Fig 103.

Fig 103: A Webley-Bentley revolver

The double-action Webley-Bentley revolvers of this pattern, were made in large numbers in both a 52 bore with a six-inch barrel and an 80 bore pocket pistol with a four-and-a-half-inch barrel.

Webley made several changes to their models in the years following 1857 but it was not until the end of the percussion era that any major change in construction took place.

That change, after 1860, was the introduction of a solid frame double-action pistol shown in Fig 104. This model had the frame forged in one while the barrel, that was made separately, screws into the frame. Very few of these revolvers were made using the percussion system before the general adoption of breech loading pistols using metallic cartridges made them obsolete.

Fig 104: Webley solid frame revolver

Next in order of sales to the Adams, Tranter and Webley was the Kerr revolver, shown in Fig 105. This pistol, like the Adams, was made by The London Armoury Company, having been patented by John Kerr in December 1858, two years after the formation of his partnership with Adams.

The principal distinguishing features of the pistol was the side hammer and the fact that the lock could be removed from the gun by removing a couple of screws. This meant that the lock could be repaired by a gunsmith without requiring factory-made spare parts. With the same concept, the revolving mechanism, which was independent of the lock action, was made as simple as possible, consisting simply of a pawl, pivoted on the back of the trigger and a cylinder-stop to hold the cylinder in the firing position.

Fig 105:   Kerr revolver with side hammer 1860

The gun was very robust in its manufacture making it one of the most dependable and easiest pistols to repair of the time. It was a five-chamber pistol of solid frame design with a rammer fitted underneath the barrel, a feature that made it necessary for the pin securing the cylinder to be inserted from the breech end. The original model patented in 1858 was a single action piece firing only from full-cock but a double-action pistol of the same design was brought out in 1859.

Although not as popular in England as other pistols it was adopted as the official weapon of the Portuguese Army, and was also used by officers of the Confederate Army during the American Civil War.

It should also be mentioned that the Beaumont-Adams revolver was also widely used by both sides in the same war and in Europe, was adopted by both the Dutch and Russian Governments.

The Deane-Harding revolver shown in Fig 106 was less successful than the ones mentioned earlier, although some were used by officers in the British army, who were required to purchase their own arms and were able to choose any gun that would take the service ammunition. Harding's patent was filed in 1858.

Fig 106:   Deane-Harding revolver.

There were some revolvers that were still being hand-made between 1850 and 1860, one being the Daw revolver and another the Harvey.

The Daw revolver, shown in Fig 107, was the successor of the Witton and Daw or Lang revolver described earlier and retained some of the features, such as the attachment of the barrel by a cross-bolt and the form of the rammer. The single-action of the Lang however was replaced by a double-action patented by C. Pryse in 1855. The pistols were in the main purchased as a self-defence weapon and came in 80 or 90 bore with four or five-inch barrels.

Fig 107: The Daw Revolver
Pembroke Fine Arms

The Harvey revolver, shown in Fig 108, was a six chamber, double-action, hammerless pistol, having a fully enclosed mechanism. One unusual feature of the Harvey pistol was the rammer, which was not permanently attached to the piece but was secured with a spring catch so that it could be easily detached. When detached from the pistol the rammer could be used as a nipple-wrench or as a turn-screw.

Fig 108:   Harvey Revolver.
Antique Arms and Armour

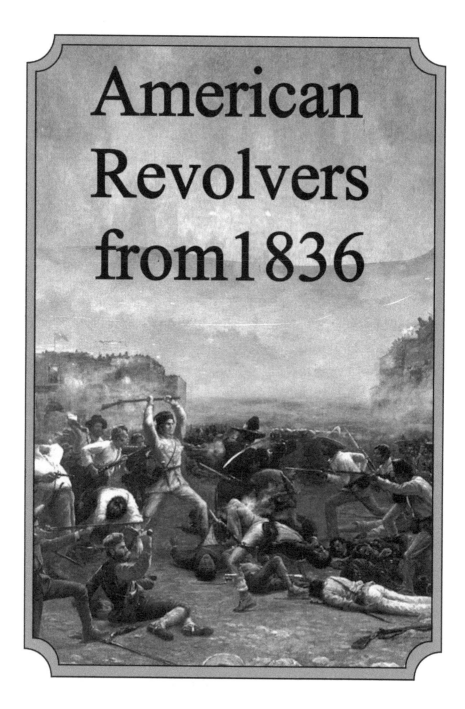

American Revolvers from 1836

Chapter 10

American Revolvers from 1836

In America, Benjamin and Barton Darling obtained a patent for a pepperbox in 1836. Theirs is the first American patent for this type of weapon and it was generally the same mechanism as was used in Europe. No early double-action lock had been patented in America, so Ethan Allen from Massachusetts was able to claim its invention in 1837.

His gun was the fastest firing pistol of the day and he became America's most prolific manufacturer of pepperbox revolvers. Fig 109 shows a presentation model Allen pepperbox revolver in its box, complete with accessories.

The pepperbox was a popular companion of the forty-niners who set out for the gold fields of California and needed help on the journey there, and later against would be claim jumpers and gold thieves.

Gamblers and dance-hall girls also found the pepperbox good protection and it is also believed that the gun was used by the United States Army in an encounter with the Cheyenne as late as 1857.

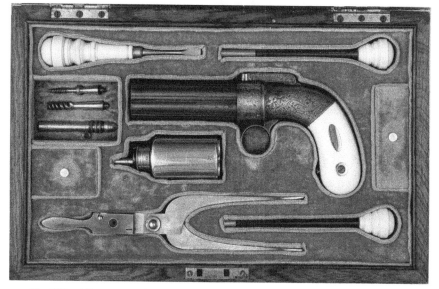

Fig 109 : Allen pepperbox revolver in its box, complete with accessories.
Metropolitan Museum of Art

The defects of the pepperbox, its lack of accuracy and tendency to fire more than one chamber at a time, have already been discussed, and Mark Twain, who was well acquainted with the gun, wrote several humorous comments about his "Allen" including.

"To aim along the turning barrel and hit the thing aimed at was a feat which was probably never done with an "Allen" in the world. But George's was a reliable weapon, nevertheless, because, as one of the stage-drivers afterward said, "If she didn't get what she went after, she would fetch something else." And so she did. She went after a deuce of spades nailed against a tree, once, and fetched a mule standing about thirty yards to the left of it. Bemis did not want the mule; but the owner came out with a double-barrelled shotgun and persuaded him to buy it, anyhow. It was a cheerful weapon—the "Allen." Sometimes all its six barrels would go off at once, and then there was no safe place in all the region round about, but behind it."

Samuel Colt

Samuel Colt reputedly came up with the idea of his famous revolver in 1830 whilst on a voyage to India at the age of sixteen. He found it a difficult and expensive task to develop his idea but he eventually took out French and English patents in 1835 and an American patent the following year.

The gun he produced, known as the Colt Paterson, was a five shot revolver with a folding trigger Fig 110. His company however failed, meaning that the pepperbox remained the dominant weapon and Colt turned his attention to other things.

Fig110: Presentation model Colt Paterson
Metropolitan Museum of Art

Some of Colt's pistols had however found their way West, where they found support amongst those who lived and fought on the frontier. There was nothing that could compare to Colt's pistol when it came to a running fight with bandits or hostile Native Americans.

In one reported incident, Captain Jack Hays and fifteen Texas Rangers, armed with Colt's revolvers, defeated seventy-five Comanches, killing over thirty of them. Even if one allows for some exaggeration on the part of the brave Rangers, it is nevertheless strong evidence for the worth of Colt's gun.

With the start of the Mexican War, Texas Rangers were mustered into United States service and the Colt enthusiasts amongst them convinced the authorities of the pistol's worth.

Captain Samuel H. Walker, who had been with Hays in the Comanche fight, was sent to find Colt and persuade him to go back into business. When Walker did manage to find Colt, he did more than just persuade him back to making his revolver. He helped re-design it, making it a stronger and more powerful weapon, Fig 111. Colt was back in business.

Fig 111: Colt Walker revolver

We have already discussed the rivalry in England between Colt and Adams and how eventually the superiority of the Adams pistol for British military use prevailed, and about the eventual closure of Colt's London factory, but Colt had serious rivals in America as well.

One very imaginative rival to Colt's revolver was the ten-shot pistol patented by Dr. Jean Alexander Francois Le Mat of New Orleans in 1856, Fig 112. Its cylinder was bored for nine chambers, that were fired in the normal way through a rifled barrel. Both .42 and .36 calibre were made. Beneath the regular barrel was a smoothbore barrel of .60 calibre loaded with buckshot. This barrel was fired by turning down the nose of the hammer.

The Le Mat revolver was a reliable weapon and with the outbreak of war the Confederacy were quick to place orders. Le Mat was dispatched to France to set up production and it wasn't long before blockade runners were carrying the guns to southern ports.

Fig 112: Ten shot revolver by LeMat
iStock

After the civil war, some guns were converted to take the new metallic cartridge but markets in Europe were limited. Several different types of cartridge had been tried and it was inevitable that the revolver would now be adapted to take it, just as single-shot pistols had done.

The metallic-cartridge firing revolver was made a reality by two Americans, Horace Smith and Daniel B. Wesson. The two men had worked together making gun barrels for Allen Brown and Luther, and had struck up a strong friendship. Smith patented a breech loading rifle in 1851 and together they perfected a repeating rifle and pistol and formed a partnership to produce the new weapons even before they obtained the patents on them in 1854. In 1855 they sold out to the Volcanic Arms Company.

Although the two men no longer worked together, the association continued. They had together developed a new improved rim-fire cartridge, and they wanted to produce a revolver that would fire it as soon as the Colt patent expired in

1857. Their gun was soon designed but there was still a problem. Their pistol needed to have the cylinder bored all the way through in order to insert the cartridge from the breech end and a patent already existed for just such a cylinder.

The patent had been obtained in 1855 by Rollin White of New Haven, Connecticut, and covered a revolver with a bored through cylinder, but of so impractical a design that the whole thing was unfeasible and there was some doubt as to whether the patent was valid.

Not wishing to test it in court, Smith and Wesson succeeded in obtaining exclusive rights to manufacture revolvers with this feature and negotiated a royalty agreement with Rollin White in 1856. This resulted in the Smith and Wesson partnership having a virtual monopoly on practical cartridge firing revolvers until 1869.

The first Smith & Wesson revolvers, Fig 113, were only of .22 calibre, and it is perhaps strange that such a small calibre gun sold so well, but at $12 per pistol and 75 cents for one hundred cartridges, it was a huge success.

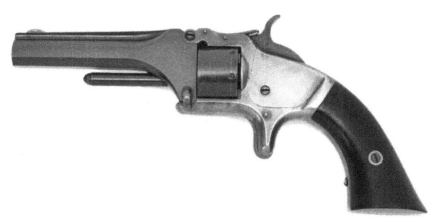

Fig 113: Smith & Wesson revolver.
Collectors Firearms

In 1860 a larger .32 calibre model was produced and this proved even more popular and served to show how much even a small calibre cartridge pistol was preferred to its percussion rival.

In 1870 George Wheeler Schofield, an officer with the 10th Cavalry, was testing the .44 American Model. Although the Army appear to have been unimpressed, Schofield was, and became an agent of the Smith & Wesson company, selling the guns in Kansas and Colorado.

Schofield also saw ways of improving the weapon and making it more robust and suitable for service on the frontier.

His input resulted in the Army purchasing over 8,000 units between 1873 and 1879. Wells Fargo and The American Express Company also decided to arm their employees with the Schofield Smith & Wesson.

The weapon was also a hit with the notorious Jesse James.

Fig 114 shows a Schofield Smith & Wesson of 1870, and as can be seen in Fig 115, it was easier to load than the earlier model where the cylinder had to be removed.

Fig 114: A Schofield patent Smith & Wesson 1870
Collectors Firearms

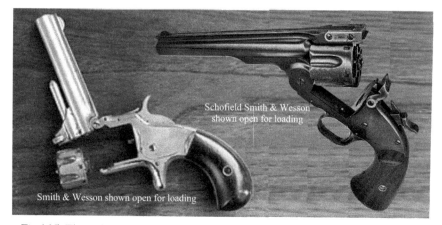

Schofield Smith & Wesson shown open for loading

Smith & Wesson shown open for loading

Fig 115: The Schofield model could be loaded without removing the cylinder

For some unknown reason Schofield chose to take his own life at Fort Apache, apparently with one of his own guns, and the heyday of Smith & Wesson was over, although the guns still sold well to markets as far away as Mexico, Russia and Turkey.

Horace Smith retired in 1873 while Daniel Wesson continued until 1883 when he took his sons into partnership.

It is remarkable that when the Rollin White patent, that had given Smith & Wesson a virtual monopoly on practical cartridge firing revolvers, expired in 1869, Colt was not ready with a competitive model. It was another four years before the new Colt Model P put in an appearance in 1873.

The Colt Model P was a single action solid fame six-shot pistol often with an ejector on the right side. The first of these pistols were .45 calibre but in 1887 a second model was introduced that took the .44-40 Winchester cartridge, meaning that anyone who wanted to arm himself with both rifle and pistol only needed one type of ammunition, Fig 116.

Fig 116: Colt model P single action revolver 1873

After the success of the model P, Colt then started to produce a number of different models with varying barrel lengths
and calibres ranging from .22 to .467. He would also offer guns
with special finishes, plating, engraving or custom grips. With
all these different models came a myriad of different names.
Colt finally introduced two double action pistols in 1877, one
a .38 calibre called the "Lightning" and the other a .41 calibre
called the "Thunderer," Billy the Kid favoured the Thunderer.
The United States army adopted a larger .45 calibre in 1878
known as the frontier model, Fig 117.

Fig 117: Colt Frontier model double action revolver 1878

One variant Colt offered was a long-barrelled variant of the
Colt Single Action Army revolver.

Many people will be familiar with the story of Wyatt Earp and his legendary Bluntline Special from films and television westerns, but exactly what type of gun Earp carried is unknown. The legend seems to stem from a best-selling, but largely fictionalized biography of Wyatt Earp, written by Stuart N. Lake in 1931.

Lake, states that the gun was noticed by Edward Z. C. Judson, a famous writer and promoter of Buffalo Bill who had the pen name of Ned Bluntline. According to Lake, Judson purchased five of guns and presented them to five western peace officers, Charley Basset, Neal Brown, Bill Tilghman, Bat Masterson and Wyatt Earp. The presentation is reputed to have taken place in Dodge City in 1877 and it is the event that gave the gun its collector's name of "Bluntline Special."

Lake describes the weapon as having a twelve inch long barrel and coming with a detachable stock, Fig 118, however there is no listing of such a weapon in Colt's catalogue, although it is possible that one could have been made as a special order.

Fig 118: Impression of a Bluntline Special as described by Lake

Whether Lake's story is fact of fiction, there is no record of such a gun being ordered by Edward Z. C. Judson or a Ned Bluntline, and no contemporary record of any presentation to lawmen taking place.

As for the standard single action colt, it was such a popular and reliable weapon that incredibly, it remained in production until 1946. General George S. Patton purchased a pair of silver plated peacemakers in 1916 and wore them during both world wars.

Later models produced after 1957 with twelve-inch barrels were called Bluntine specials, possible as a marketing ploy, Fig 119.

Fig 119:   Bluntline Special 1957
National Firearms Museum

The British breech loading revolver

Chapter 11

The British Breech-loading Revolver

The first English-made breech-loading revolver would appear to have been a pirated imitation of the rim-fire Smith & Wesson shown in Fig 113. It was made in the late fifties or early sixties and is attributed to Webley, although the maker preferred to remain anonymous for obvious reasons. The revolver itself was an exact copy of the Smith & Wesson gun, single-action, seven chambered and .22 calibre, the only difference being the absence of any maker's mark on the weapon.

It was not until Tranter, the originator of the double trigger, took out a patent on a rimfire breech loading revolver in 1863 that the system caught on in England. The Tranter breech loader, Fig 120, was similar in form to the earlier double action, a solid frame, single trigger percussion revolver of 1856.

This breech loader however had six cylinders and a loading gate on the right-hand side for loading the cartridges into the chambers. It also had an ejector adapted from the rammer of the earlier gun that could be used to push the spent cartridges out, one at a time.

Fig 120: Tranter breech loading revolver with loading gate and ejector.

Tranter produced several versions of the gun, with different calibres including a .450, .442 and .380 calibre, there was also a pocket revolver of either .320 or .22 calibre which resembled the larger gun but was not fitted with an ejector.

Also produced at the time was a single action pocket revolver with seven .320 calibre chambers Fig 121.

The gun had a sheath trigger with no trigger guard and a three-and-a-half-inch barrel.

The next development in English revolvers came with the introduction of the Boxer centre-fire cartridge in 1867.

Introduction of the Boxer cartridge was followed later that same year by a breech loading revolver patented by John Adams, the brother of Robert Adams and a partner in the London Armoury Company.

Fig 121:   Tranter seven shot .320 calibre single action pocket revolver

The new pistol, a solid frame, .450 calibre, six-chamber gun with a six-inch barrel, was adopted by the British Government as a replacement for the Beaumont-Adams percussion revolver. It had a loading gate on the right-hand side and used a short Boxer pistol cartridge. The empty cases were removed with a fixed rod that operated in a guide fixed to the frame. See Fig 122.

Fig 122:   John Adams patent centre-fire six shot revolver 1867

Adams severed his connection with The London Arms Company when his revolver was adopted by the Government and formed a new Company, the "Adams Patent Small Arms Company" to produce it.

The adoption of the Adams breech loading revolver seemed to signal the general adoption of the Boxer cartridge for most, if not all, breech loaders, including a new Tranter centre-fire revolver as well as a new large calibre Webley Fig 123.

Fig 123: Webley No1 solid frame .577 centre-fire 1866

The Webley accepted a .577 calibre Boxer cartridge with a reduced charge. It had a double-action mechanism identical to that of the Tranter revolver but sported only a four-inch barrel. The breech end of the cylinder was covered by a steel plate which revolved with it and was pierced with six holes corresponding to the positions of the caps in the centre-fire cartridges contained in the chambers.

The steel plate was designed to prevent the gun being jammed by defective cartridges, a not uncommon fault with the early Boxer ammunition, were the cap could bulge outwards on being fired and jam against the frame of the pistol. The draw-back was that it made it necessary to remove the cylinder and its breech shield in order to reload, and for that reason its use was discontinued in later models in favour of a loading gate and an ejector rod that was housed in a recess in the cylinder pin when not in use.

Webley revolvers of the new pattern were made in both .450 and .442 calibre with barrels ranging from two-and-a-half to four-and-a-half inch in length, the best known being the R.I.C. revolver made for the Royal Irish Constabulary, and the double action pocket pistol known as the Bulldog Fig 124.

Fig 124: Webley R.I.C. pistol (top image) and Webley Bulldog
(bottom image)
Royal Armouries

Although the centre-fire cartridge effectively made non-breech loading weapons obsolete, there was nevertheless a brief overlapping of the two systems between 1865 and 1870. It is probably just the human trait of not wanting to plunge into something so new and burning bridges, that saw a few manufacturers at this time produce a range of dual-system revolvers with interchangeable cylinders, one percussion and one cartridge taking.

A Footnote

The years between 1868 and 1883, during which the Adams revolver was the standard British service revolver, saw a great many small campaigns. The Abyssinian campaign in 1868, the Ashantee Expedition in 1878, the second Afghan war in 1878, the Zulu War 1879 and the Egyptian Campaign of 1882. The Egyptian Campaign led into a series of campaigns against the Dervishes of the Sudan, who had risen in revolt under the leadership of the Mahdi. The Mahdi saw himself as appointed by God for the utter destruction of the Infidel, and vowed to spread fire, sword and the true religion throughout the whole of Egypt.

The Mahdi's followers were fanatics who fought with great ferocity and absolute disregard for their own lives. Against such a foe, many British officers felt that the Adams revolver fell short, proving incapable of stopping a charging fanatic at point-blank range.

As a consequence, there was a tendency for officers, serving against the Dervishes, to abandon the revolver in favour of a large double-barrelled saddle-pistol made by Thomas Horsley or the Lancaster four barrelled pistol shown in Fig 125. The later had four fixed barrels and a revolving firing-pin. The pistol shown has a double action identical to the early Tranter revolvers, a feature that enabled them to be fired from full-cock. The breech loading system of this pistol is of the hinged, "drop down" type operated by a side lever. The pistol also ejected the spent cartridges as the gun was broken open for loading.

Pistols of this type were found to shoot more strongly and have greater stopping power than the equivalent calibre revolver, owing to the absence of the escape of gas between the barrel and the cylinder, an unavoidable defect of the revolving weapon. The standard model, shown earlier in Fig 74, had a single trigger but they were sometime fitted with a Tranter type double trigger, as shown here, to help with the heavy pull required for the double action.

Fig 125: Four barrelled pistol by Lancaster 1879 with Tranter type trigger

Automatic Ejectors

The first English revolver to have an automatic ejection system was the Thomas revolver patented in 1869. The barrel and cylinder slid forward and the empty cartridges were withdrawn by a star-shaped extractor that remained fixed to the breech.

To eject the cartridges, it was necessary to press a catch in front of the trigger guard and give a turn to a bolt fixed upon the underside of the barrel, which drew the cylinder forward, released the spent cartridges and pulled the barrel away from the frame of the gun. Before reloading the barrel and cylinder had to be returned to their original position so that the new ammunition could be inserted through a loading gate on the righthand side of the breech.

This system of ejection had only a short life-span however, because its introduction coincided with the introduction of a far superior system by Smith & Wesson in America.

This system was patented in 1869 and combined a breech loading system of the hinged frame type and the use of a ratchet operated "star ejector" which was fixed upon the end of a rod passing through a hollow in the cylinder-pin and was operated by the act of breaking the pistol open.

As the pistol was opened, the star ejector popped the spent cartridges out and snapped back when the pistol was fully open for loading, with the barrel pointing down.

The introduction of the pistol into England during the early seventies was closely followed in 1876 by that of a Webley pistol patented by C. Pryse and commonly known as the Pryse Army revolver. Fig 126 shows the Webley-Pryse revolver with an inset of the gun broken open for loading with the ejector system exposed.

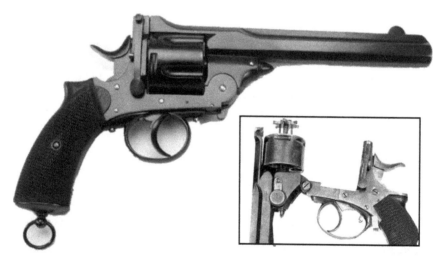

Fig 126: A Webley-Pryse revolver with an inset of the gun broken open for loading with the ejector system exposed.

The Webley-Pryse revolver was never officially adopted by the government, but it does seem to have been tolerated as an alternative to the Adams as a service pistol and was widely used by officers between its introduction in 1876 and the final replacement of the Adams revolver in 1882.

The replacement for the Adams was the breech loading Enfield revolver, so called because it was manufactured at the Government small arms factory in Enfield Fig 127. This was a double action pistol with a "rebounding lock," that is to say, that when the trigger is released after firing the hammer is automatically raised to the half-cock safety position.

Fig 127: Enfield breech loading revolver
Royal Armouries

The Enfield revolver had an unusual breech loading and extracting mechanism patented by O. Jones, an employee at Enfield, in 1876. It consisted of a hinged barrel and a sliding cylinder. The cylinder slid along a rigid cylinder-pin screwed into the breech of the pistol and was fitted with a fixed extractor. Loading was achieved by means of a hinged cylinder-gate on the righthand side of the pistol.

This somewhat clumsy arrangement seems to have been adopted by the military, because it was felt, mistakenly, that the Smith & Wesson or Webley type of extraction system would not be robust or reliable enough for service life.

The same year that saw the government Enfield revolver introduced also saw a new and improved Webley revolver and during the years 1883 and 1887 the Webley proved to be a much more popular and superior weapon and the War Office was forced to admit it had made a mistake with the Enfield, and placed an order for some 10,000 of the new Mk 1 Webley. The placing of the order was quickly followed by the official adoption of the Mk 11 Webley in 1889 Fig 128.

Mark 1 Webley

Mark 11 Webley

Fig 128: Webley revolvers Mk 1 and Mk 11

Another type of breech loading system for revolvers was the solid frame swing-out mechanism, first introduced by Colt in 1889 as the Colt double action Navy revolver. The cylinder was locked by a catch on the left-hand side which when disengaged, allowed the cylinder to swing out to the left on a pivoted crane Fig 129.

The spent cartridges were ejected manually with a spring-loaded ejector. The colt system was successful enough to inspire emulation and the first Smith & Wesson with a swing-out cylinder appeared in 1896. Smith & Wesson went on to produce a wide range of swing-out cylinder models, as did Colt in later years.

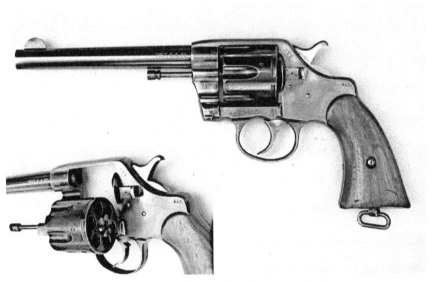

Fig 129: Colt revolver with swing-out cylinder

The Magazine Repeater

Chapter 12

The Magazine Repeater

The date of the invention of the first repeater to make use of a magazine is unknown. Once again, the Diarist Samuel Pepys gives a clue but only to the fact that such weapons had been developed before the entry in his diary for the 3rd July 1662. In it he states that, *"I examined a gun to discharge seven times, the best of all devices I ever saw, and very serviceable, and not a bawble; for it is much approved of and many made."*

There is nothing in his diary to indicate what sort of gun he saw, but it is assumed by many students to have been one of the two principal repeaters of the time, ether the Kalthoff or the Lorenzoni. Although these weapons are attributed to the two mentioned gunsmiths there is no actual evidence that they were the inventors.

There were several in the gunsmiths in the Kalthoff family although we do not know how they were related. Various members of the family were granted patents for similar magazine repeating guns in France and the Netherlands in 1640 and 1641 respectively but it is not certain that a Kalthoff invented it. It wasn't long before gunsmiths in England and other places could and did make similar arms.

The early Wheellock Kalthoff repeater had two magazines, one for powder and another for balls. A carrier large enough for one charge is attached to the pivoted trigger guard. A forward and backward movement of the guard turned the breech chamber so that it received a ball from one magazine and powder from the other.

Later flintlock examples such as Fig 130, varied with different makers, but all had a revolving breech chamber. The position of the magazines varied, sometimes being in the butt and sometimes under the lock.

A gun of that nature, at that time, created a lot of interest and they were made throughout Europe. The disadvantage of the weapon was its intricacy, as it was an expensive gun to produce and could only be repaired by a skilled gunsmith. The gunpowder had to be kept very dry to run smoothly in the lock and the gun required a lot of maintenance to prevent fouling.

Fig 130: Typical Kalthoff flintlock repeater

The Lorenzoni system Fig 131, had all the same advantages and disadvantages of the Kalthoff.

There were two magazines in the stock, one for powder and one for balls and there was a third attached to the lock for priming powder.

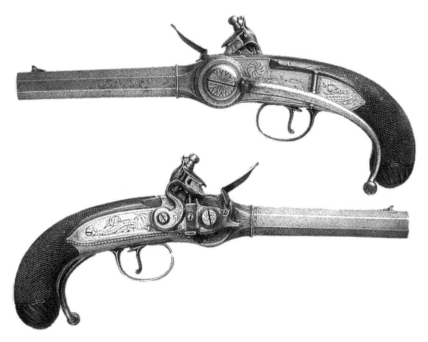

Fig 131: Lorenzoni magazine loader.
Metropolitan Museum of Art

To load the gun the shooter held it with the barrel pointed up and pulled back a lever located on the left side. This rotated the breech-block so that the two cavities in it lined up with the magazine openings in the stock, see Fig 132.

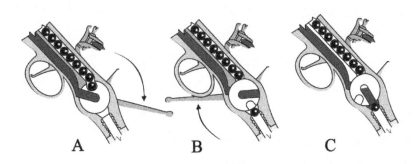

Fig 132: A Breech block receives ball and powder. B Breech block delivers ball to chamber. C Breech block delivers powder to chamber

The shooter then pointed the barrel down, filling the cavities with one charge of powder and one ball, he then returned the lever to its original position, thus carrying first the ball and then the powder forward to the chamber. At the same time the motion of the lever primed the pan and cocked the gun.

There is some evidence that there were accidents caused by the block not fitting tightly enough or the shooter not locking it in the proper position, resulting in flame leaking back from the chamber and igniting the powder in the magazine. An accident that could easily cause serious injury or even prove fatal for the unfortunate shooter.

Guns with the loading system just described were made by Lorenzoni in Florence during the mid-seventieth century which is why it carries his name, but it is likely the system was devised earlier. The guns were made for some time and even found their way to America where it was manufactured by John Pim of Boston around 1722 and by John Cookson who also lived near Boston, and advertised the gun in the Boston Gazette in 1756. However, as long as powder and ball had to be loaded separately there were always going to be difficulties constructing a safe reliable repeater until the advent of the modern cartridge.

Enter onto the stage one Walter Hunt, a mechanic and inventor. Born in upstate New York, he moved to Brooklyn in 1826 where he devised a flax-spinning machine, a spring trap, an iceboat, a heating stove, a nail making machine, fountain pen, safety-pin and a sewing machine. He failed however to capitalise on his inventions and died a poor man.

With such a brain at that time it was almost inevitable that he would look at improving firearms, and indeed he did, patenting both a new bullet in 1848 and a gun to fire it. The bullet consisted of a conventional looking outer shape with a cavity in the base to hold the powder charge. The cavity was sealed with a cork plug that had a hole through the centre to admit the flash from the primer Fig 133.

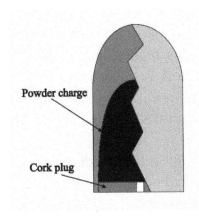

Powder charge

Cork plug

Fig 133: Hunt's bullet

Hunt's bullet was strong enough to be pushed along a tubular magazine by a spring and that was the basis for Hunt's rifle.

He designed a rifle with a tubular magazine sited beneath the barrel and devised a straight-drive firing-pin activated by a spiral spring.

The design was years ahead of anything else at the time but his repeating mechanism was too delicate to be practical and needed work.

Hunt had neither the capital nor the business skills to take the project further and assigned his rights to George Arrowsmith, a New York machinist. A mechanic at the Arrowsmith plant by the name of Lewis Jennings simplified Hunt's mechanism and obtained an additional patent. Arrowsmith then sold the Hunt and Jennings patents to Courtland Palmer. In 1850 Palmer arranged for the guns to be manufactured by Robbins & Lawrence in Windsor, Vermont.

The gun now came to the attention of Horace Smith and Daniel Wesson. They improved the weapon still further and took out additional patents. By 1854, they had in their hands a very superior weapon. Smith, Wesson and Palmer formed a partnership and established a factory at Norwich, Connecticut, however within a year the partners sold their interests to a group of New York and New Haven capitalists.

The new corporation of forty investors included clockmakers, carriage manufacturers, bakers, grocers and men from the world of shipping.

One name however, stands out from those of the rest, a shirt manufacturer from New Haven by the name of Oliver F. Winchester.

Winchester may not have known a great deal about firearms but he knew about business and his original eighty shares gradually grew to a controlling interest in the company. The "Volcanic Repeating Arms Company" now produced rifles and pistols of the pattern developed by Smith & Wesson along with the ammunition.

The ammunition differed from Hunt's original design insofar as the hollow in the base of the bullet was now filled with a percussion compound as well as gunpowder, making the cartridge self-contained. Daniel Wesson patented an improved centre-fire cartridge in 1854 and the Volcanic Repeating Arms Company obtained the rights to his patent, along with other assets, when they bought out Smith Wesson and Palmer, but for some reason it never used the Wesson cartridge.

Financial problems forced the company into bankruptcy in 1857 and the assets were purchased by Oliver F. Winchester. He called the new company "New Haven Arms Company" and installed himself as president. Winchester devoted himself to financial matters and placed Benjamin Tyler Henry as manager of the New Haven plant.

The new company was soon in trouble and something had to be done. In 1858 Winchester set Henry the task of designing a new cartridge that would be more powerful than the previous one, but still be safe and self-contained. It didn't take long for Henry to design a .44 rim-fire metal cased cartridge, and alter the Volcanic arm so that it could be used. At the same time, he modified the locking bolt and redesigned the firing-pin so that it struck both sides of the cartridge rim at once, lessoning the chances of a misfire.

The new rifle and its ammunition was a complete success. To operate the new gun Fig 134, it was first loaded by compressing a long spiral spring located in the cylindrical magazine beneath the barrel until the front section could be swung to the side. It was then possible to load fifteen cartridges into the main magazine. As the front section was swung back into place the spring kept the newly loaded cartridges under pressure.

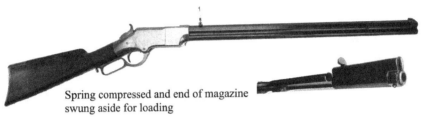

Spring compressed and end of magazine
swung aside for loading

Fig 134: Henry rifle showing method of loading

A quick forwards and backwards movement of the trigger guard carried a cartridge from the magazine into the chamber and cocked the gun ready for firing.

Government tests showed that an experienced shooter could fire one hundred and twenty rounds in three hundred and forty seconds, or one shot every 2.9 seconds, even allowing for loading. Some shooters, not content with fifteen shots would carry one cartridge ready in the chamber giving him sixteen shots before having to reload.

The Henry rifle was ready for sale in 1862 and Winchester had several silver-plated, presentation arms produced, two of which were given to the Secretary of the Navy, Gideon Welles, and the Secretary of War, Simon Cameron.

Winchester could well have expected a large government order to follow but he was disappointed; the Chief of Ordinance was Brigadier General James Wolfe Ripley.

Ripley was reluctant to adopt a new arm, worried that it may have teething problems and he also worried that soldiers would waste ammunition given a weapon that could fire so often. He was confident in what the Springfield could accomplish, so in the end only some 1700 of the new Henrys were purchased.

However disappointed Winchester was by the lack of government orders, he was delighted by the response from Kentucky and Missouri which saw both state and private purchases, boosted no doubt by a popular tale of the time.

The story goes that Captain James M. Wilson of Kentucky was eating dinner with his family when seven guerrilla fighters burst in and started firing wildly.

Pleading with them to spare his family, Wilson persuaded them to take him outside to be shot. Once outside he ran, amid a hail of poorly aimed bullets, to an outhouse.

The tale continues... *"Several shots passed through his hat and more through his clothing, but none took effect upon his person. He thus reached his cover and seized his Henry rifle, turned it upon his foes, and in five shots killed five of them; the other two sprung for their horses. As the sixth man threw his hand over the pommel of his saddle, the sixth shot took off four of his fingers; notwithstanding this he got into his saddle, but the seventh shot killed him; then starting out, Capt. Wilson killed the seventh man with the eighth shot."*

The tale states that as a consequence of Wilson's heroic action his company was armed with Henry rifles.

Whether the tale is true or not, Wilson's men and other units were armed with Henrys and sales were good. In 1866 Oliver Winchester got out of the shirt-making business and devoted himself full-time to a re-organised corporation, now called "The Winchester Repeating Arms Company" and a new improved rifle, named the Winchester rifle Model 1866 was produced, Fig 135, with a forestock and loading gate. The loading gate ment that the magazine could be a solid tube and no longer open on the underside as the earlier Henry rifles had been.

Fig 135:   Winchester Rifle model 1866
National Firearms Museum

While the Henry was a very successful repeating rifle it was not the only one, or even the first. That title went to the seven-shot repeater invented by Christopher M. Spencer of Connecticut, patented on March 6th, 1860, seven months before the Henry.

The Spencer rifle Fig 136, carried seven cartridges that were kept in a tubular magazine in the stock. It had a lever action that carried the cartridges from the magazine in the stock to the chamber and then ejected each after it had been fired. It was not self-cocking like the Henry and held less shots, but it was simpler, sturdier and cheaper.

When war broke out in 1861 Spencer's new rifle was the first to be offered to the federal government. The navy ordered a number of the rifles, but Spencer met with the same response from Ripley and the army as Winchester had done.

Abraham Lincoln however, owned a Spencer of his own and ordered Ripley to place an order for the gun in December 1861.

There were some problems at first with production, and that, along with Ripley still trying to limit the order, meant that the gun didn't make its presence felt until 1863.

Fig 136:   The Spencer repeater rifle

Regiments at the front were crying out for the gun, with many using their own money to purchase the weapon but Riply still continued to delay.

Spencer approached Lincoln and arranged a personal demonstration of the gun, with which Lincoln was already familiar, and within two weeks Ripley was fired and there was a new Chief of Ordinance.

The gun was a huge success and it is possible that in the third year of the war, as many as two hundred thousand Spencer rifles were in use.

After the war, orders naturally declined and refinements were added such as a cutoff that allowed the gun to be used as a single-shot weapon while still holding a full magazine in reserve. But the Spencer could not compete with the Winchester Model 1866 in the civilian marketplace and in 1869, The Spencer Repeating Rifle Company was dissolved and its assets sent for auction.

The two biggest purchasers of the Spencer company assets were the Turkish government, which purchase thirty thousand guns, and Oliver Winchester, who now had no credible rival.

There was no doubt about the performance of lever action magazine repeaters on the battlefield. The civil war and its use on the western plains proved it to Americans. The slaughter of the attacking Russian armies by Turks armed with Winchesters at Plevna in 1877, proved it to the rest of the world.

European experts were aware of the fact that the lever action worked well with metallic cartridges, but they much preferred the bolt action, for one thing, it was easier to operate by a man lying prone on the ground than was the lever action, and many European gun makers were developing bolt action repeating rifles before the end of the American Civil War.

Frederick Vetteri of Switzerland had looked closely at both the Henry and Winchester arms, and developed a bolt-action rifle with a tubular magazine under the barrel, a cartridge carrier similar to the Henry model, and a loading gate adopted from one of Nelson Kings improvements to the 1866 Winchester Fig 137.

Fig 137:   Vetterli bolt-action rifle Model 1870

In Austria, Ferdinand Früwirth designed a similar rifle which was adopted by the gendarmerie in 1869. In Germany, Peter Paul Mauser of Oberdorf designed a single shot bolt-action rifle in the late 1860s and developed a repeater with a tube magazine under the barrel in 1884, but these guns were no more than a transition.

James P. Lee, a Scottish watchmaker who had obtained United States citizenship, designed a box magazine that was located directly below the bolt Fig 138, and it was adopted by the Navy in 1879 and the idea had spread world-wide within ten years.

Fig 138: Lee-Metfort with box magazine beneath the bolt

Completely independently of Lee, Ferdinand Ritter von Mannlicher also invented a box-magazine in 1882, and he improved the design in 1883 and 84. In 1885 he designed a cartridge-clip. The cartridge-clip allowed a magazine load of cartridges to be fastened together in advance and loaded in a single motion. Most clips after that date were simply variants of Mannlicher's design.

The repeater rifle now had two really successful and reliable systems to choose from; lever action and bolt action, and a third, with a sliding action called a pump-action, was on its way.

In 1895 a new rifle was adopted in Britain, although the Lee-Enfield was really a redesign of the Lee-Metford it saw service from 1895 until 1957. The world war one versions were often referred to as the SMLE which is short for the, Short Magazine Lee-Enfield or simply as the three-o-three Fig 139. It featured a ten round magazine that was loaded with .303 British cartridges. Although officially replaced in 1957 some commonwealth countries still kept it in service until much later. Total production of all Lee-Enfield rifles is estimated at over 17 million units!

Fig 139: Lee-Enfield rifle

Chapter 13

Self-loading pistols (Semi-Automatic)

Although the development of the metallic cartridge and smokeless powder did not cause any major technical advance in revolver design, they did herald the arrival of automatic systems, that is the use of some of the energy, generated by the discharge of the weapon, to reload and re-cock for the next shot.

It should be explained that, what is now generally referred to as an "automatic pistol," is in fact, a self-loading or semi-automatic weapon, the term automatic in its fullest sense only referring to machine guns, where the weapon will continue to fire as long as the trigger is depressed.

It would take an entire other book to describe the various automatic systems, let alone the different types and designs of guns that have employed them, but for historical reason, some do require a mention, and first it may be that some explanation of the different types of self-loading actions is necessary.

Actions

When a gun is discharged the expanding gases push in both directions, every action having an equal and opposite reaction. In a non-self-loading weapon all the forward force is used to expel the bullet from the barrel, and the backward force is absorbed by the frame of the gun and the hand of the shooter, hence the kick.

With a self-loading gun, some of the force is used to push the spent cartridge case and breech-block back, so that the spent cartridge can be ejected from the breech. There are basically three types of action that use recoil for the purpose of ejecting the spent cartridge, loading a new cartridge in the chamber and cocking the gun ready to fire the next shot. There are many variations but the basics are:

Blowback:

This action uses the weight of the slide/breechblock and the hammer to delay the opening of the breech until the bullet has exited the muzzle, and pressure in the chamber has dropped to a safe level. The weight of the slide/breechblock allows the spent cartridge case to move backwards immediately but not so fast that dangerous pressures escape.

Locked-breech:

This action is used when the pressure in the chamber would be so high that the opening of the breech would occur too quickly. With this action, the slide/breechblock and the barrel are locked together for a short distance. When the gun is fired the slide/breechblock and the barrel travel backwards together for a short distance, but at some point, when the pressure has dropped, the barrel will encounter a lug that will disengage it from the slide/breechblock, which will then con-tinue back alone, opening the breech and ejecting the spent cartridge case.

Delayed blowback:

This is used where recoil is not powerful enough to warrant a locked-breech. Sometimes a spring lever is used to increase the resistance of the slide/breechblock to keep the case in the chamber long enough to be safe.

Fig 140 shows the basic sequence of a semi-automatic action.

Sequence of semi-automatic fire

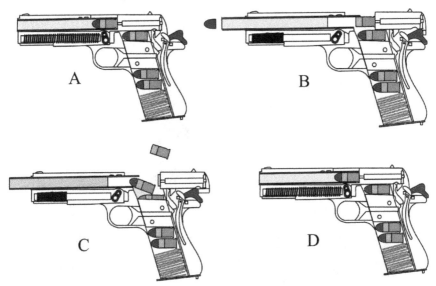

A Gun cocked and ready to fire
B Gun discharged, breech begins to open
C Spent cartridge ejected and new round loading
D New round loaded, breech closed and gun cocked for next shot

Fig 140:   Sequence of semi-automatic fire

Many attempts were made to manufacture a revolver with an automatic ejection system without success, but one, more properly referred to as a self-cocking revolver, was the Webley-Fosbery system manufactured by Webley & Scott. See Fig 101.

The barrel and cylinder of this pistol were free to slide in a grooved guide in such a manner that, upon the gun being fired, they recoiled independently of the butt for about three-quarters of an inch. This recoil action served to raise the hammer to the full-cock position where it was retained by the sear, and partially rotated the cylinder. As the barrel and cylinder were returned to their original position by coil spring, the rotation of the cylinder was completed and the gun was ready for its next shot.

The actual rotation of the cylinder was achieved with the aid of a stud operating in the zig-zag grooves that can be seen on the exterior of the cylinder.

Fig 141: Webley-Fosbery self-cocking pistol
National Firearms Museum

The breech-loading and extracting mechanisms of the Fosbery automatic revolver were the same as those of the Webley Mk.V1, the empty cases being ejected by the action of opening the breech and new cartridges being inserted one at a time by hand, a system that compared unfavourably with the magazine-loading system of other automatic pistols, but which enabled it to use the .455 revolver cartridge, instead of the special rimless ammunition.

The first practical self-loading pistol was the Austrian Schonberger made in 1892 Fig 142. The gun has a fixed magazine situated just in front of the trigger guard. It takes a Mannlicher type of clip and has a locked breech.

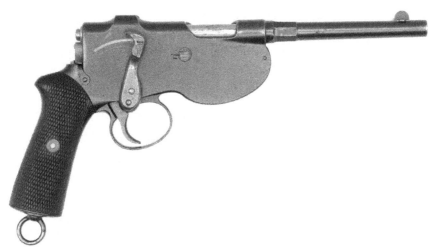

Fig 142: Austrian Schonberger
National Firearms Museum

Next to appear on the scene was the Borchardt in 1893 Fig 143.

Fig 143:   Borchardt pistol 1893

This pistol is important historically because it was the first to use a detachable magazine inserted into the butt of the pistol from below. he breech was locked by a toggle link, also used in the more famous Luger-Parabellum.

The first pocket automatic, (I will use the simple term "automatic" from now on to mean any self-loading or semi-automatic pistol,) was produced by Theodore Bergmann in 1894, followed by two military automatics that appeared in 1897 and 1903.

The magazine on all the early Bergmann pistols was just ahead of the trigger guard and access to it was by means of a pivoted side plate. The cartridges were held in a light clip that was withdrawn by means of small loop after the side plate was closed Fig 144.

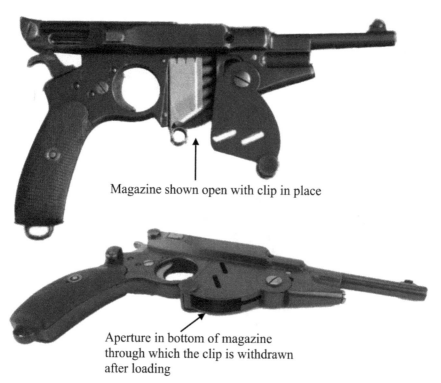

Magazine shown open with clip in place

Aperture in bottom of magazine
through which the clip is withdrawn
after loading

Fig 144: Bergmann automatic 1894-1903

A clip that is withdrawn from the magazine after loading is often referred to a "stripper clip," as opposed to a Mannlicher clip that remains in the magazine until the last round has been fired.

Some models of the Bergmann were fitted with extractors but some weren't. Because of this practice some cartridges were rimless or grooved and some had neither rims nor grooves.

Another very successful automatic pistol was the Mauser pistol of 1898. The Mauser was the pistol carried by Winston Churchill at the battle of Omdurman in 1898 Fig 145.

Fig 145:   Mauser automatic 1898

The Mauser came with an attachable shoulder stock to turn it into a carbine, and it was the first to feature something that is now considered essential for military purposes, that being a breech that remains open when the last cartridge has been fired. This feature prevents the embarrassment of presenting an empty weapon to an adversary in the mistaken believe that it still has a round to fire.

One name that is synonymous with automatic pistols is Browning, as John Moses Browning was amongst the most successful and prolific firearm inventors. Born in Ogden, Utah in 1855 he designed rifles and pistols for the likes of Winchester, Remington and Colt and during his life, held more than a hundred and twenty patents for firearm mechanism designs.

By 1900 Browning had developed two types of automatic pistol, one for low-powered cartridges, using a straight blowback action and the other a short-recoil locked-action for high powered cartridges.

The blow-back pistol was made by Fabrique National of Liége, Belgium. As with all Browning designed pistols the magazine was in the butt, however with this pistol, the slide-spring was mounted above the barrel, giving the impression of two barrels Fig 146.

Fig 146:   Browning blow-back pistol 1900
The Royal Armouries Collection

John Moses Browning was inventive, even as a child. He made his first gun in his father's gun shop at the age of thirteen and in 1879 he patented a self-cocking single shot rifle that he and his brother sold to the Winchester Repeating Arms Company. Among his more famous designs are the Winchester Model 1886 lever-action rifle, the Remington model 1905 semi-automatic shotgun, the Colt Model 1911 semi-automatic pistol and the Over-and-under shotgun made by Fabrique National of Belgium.

The Browning automatic rifle was adopted by the U.S. Army in 1918 and U.S. forces used Browning automatic and semi-automatic weapons almost exclusively until the 1980s.

Another famous semi-automatic pistol that Hollywood has made us all familiar with, is the Luger, manufactured by Waffen-und Munitionsfabriken. The pistol, as well as the parabellum cartridge that it was designed to take, was invented by George Luger in 1898 and has a toggle action, as opposed to the slide action used by almost every other semi-automatic pistol. A Luger pistol from 1918 is shown in Fig 147, together with an inset that shows the breech open.

The Luger or Parabellum pistol was standard issue to German officers during both world wars. The name Parabellum comes from the Latin, "If you want peace, prepare for war."

With the toggle action, after a round is fired, the barrel and toggle assembly (which have been locked together at this point), travel rearward due to the recoil. After moving roughly 13 mm (0.5 in) rearward, the toggle strikes a cam built into the frame, causing the knee joint to hinge and the toggle and breech assembly to unlock.

At this point the barrel impacts the frame and stops its rearward movement, but the toggle assembly continues moving and bends at the knee joint due to momentum, extracting the spent casing from the chamber and ejecting it. The toggle and breech assembly subsequently travel forward under spring tension and the next round from the magazine is loaded into the chamber.

Fig 147: Luger pistol 1918

This mechanism works well for higher-pressure cartridges, but lower pressure can cause the pistol to malfunction because they do not generate enough recoil to work the action fully. This results in either the breech block not clearing the top cartridge of the magazine or becoming jammed open on the cartridge's base. While this type of malfunction with under-powered cartridges can and does occur with other pistol designs, the Luger tends to be quite sensitive to changes in ammunition.

Advances in self-loading pistol design have continued but these are really beyond the scope of this book and the reader is encouraged to seek more specialised publications.

A Little about Webley & Scott

Webley's first autoloading pistol was an experimental .45 calibre pistol produced in 1903 but the first mass-produced model was the .32 ACP model in 1906.

Webley & Scott pistols were produced in a range of bores from .22 inch to .455 inch, and included 9 mm models, all of which were single-action blowback pistols, designed by William Whiting. Production ceased in 1940.

In 1905, Webley had presented an auto-loading pistol for testing by the Small Arms Committee, a British military group charged with organizing trials and making recommendations of arms to the War Office. The SAC, which had begun testing automatics in 1900, was unimpressed by Webley's offering, preferring foreign automatics including the Colt.

However, no automatic was recommended over contemporary service revolvers, which were all Webleys at the time, and trials would continue until 1913.

In 1910 a new automatic was tested, and in 1911 the Webley self-loading .455-inch Mark I was recommended by both the SAC and the Chief Inspector of Small Arms.

This pistol was adopted by the Royal Navy in early 1912 as the first automatic pistol officially in British service. Later the pistol was also adopted by the Royal Horse Artillery and was issued to members of the Royal Flying Corps.

The Webley & Scott semi-automatic .455 pistol had a 7-round magazine. It was rugged and accurate at short range, but also heavy with an awkward grip angle Fig 148.

It was prone to jamming throughout most of its service career, owing largely to its cordite ammunition, which left residue that fouled the close tolerances of its diagonally locking breech. The problem was officially resolved in 1914 with the introduction of the Mark IZ (nitrocellulose) cartridge.

Fig 148:   Webley & Scott .455 Mk.1
National Firearms Museum

Fig 149: Webley & Scott .32 ACP Pistol

Although never officially adopted by the British Army, Webley self-loaders were popular as back-up or personal weapons by British and Commonwealth personnel in both World Wars.

The 1906 Webley & Scott semi-automatic .32 ACP pistol was adopted by the London Metropolitan Police in 1911, and is sometimes referred to as the Webley MP for this reason, Fig 149.

The Machine Gun

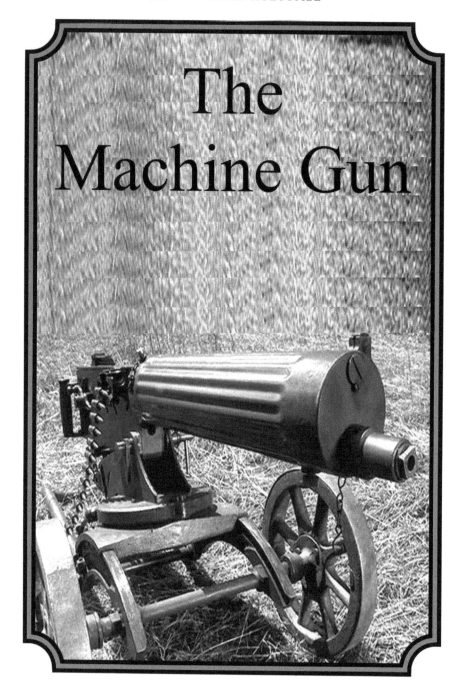

Chapter 14

The Machine-gun

Probably the first really successful rapid-fire weapons were the Agar Gun and the Gatling gun, that put in an appearance in 1861 and 1862, however neither of these guns would actually fit todays definition of a machine gun because they were not fully automatic, having to be powered by turning a crank by hand, but it's a good place to start.

The Agar Gun.

Sometimes referred to as the Coffee-mill because of its resemblance to one, the Agar gun Fig 150, was invented by Wilson Agar at the beginning of the American Civil War. This gun featured a loading system linking a hand crank to a hopper above. It used paper cartridges fitted with a percussion cap that were inserted into metal tubes that acted as chambers. The gun was demonstrated to President Lincoln in 1861. The President was impressed and the Union Army purchase 54 guns but they saw only limited act

Fig 150: The Agar gun

The Gatling gun.

Patented in 1861, the Gatling gun Fig 151, was the first gun to offer controlled sequential firing with automatic loading of prepared cartridges. It was operated by use of a hand crank and saw some limited service action in the American Civil War.

The Gatling Gun had some later improvements and saw service in the Franco-Prussian War of 1870. Many guns were sold to other armies in the late nineteenth century and it continued to be used into the early twentieth. The large wheels that were required for transport gave it a high firing position that made it and its crew vulnerable to both snipers and artillery. It later gave way to the Maxim gun.

Fig 151: The Gatling Gun

The Maxim gun.

The Maxim gun, Fig 152, was invented by Sir Hiram Maxim and was the first self-powered machine gun using the power of the recoil of the previous shot to reload, rather than a hand-operated crank. Maxim also introduced the use of a water jacket to cool the gun which would became hot due to the rapid rate of fire. Trials showed that the Maxim gun could fire 500 rounds per minute or the equivalent of 30 bolt action rifles.

The Maxim gun was developed in the 1880s at the high point of British and European imperialism, and was first used by the British in the First Matabele War of 1893-1894. It is said that in one engagement 50 British soldiers fought off 5.000 warriors with just four Maxim Guns, prompting Hilaire Belloc to write, *"Whatever happens, we have got, the Maxim gun and they have not."*

Fig 152:   The Maxim Gun Mk1 1892

The Maxim was widely adopted and derivative designs were used on all sides during the First World War. The First Wold War showed the importance of the machine gun on the battlefield, as can be seen from the fact that the United States Army issued four machine guns per regiment in 1912 but increased that to three hundred and thirty six per regiment in 1919.

Although the British had been among the first nations to adopt the machine-gun, it entered World War1 under equipped with the weapon. The French also seemed to have largely underestimated the dominance it would have on the battlefield. The Germans on the other hand, put great store in the weapon, and the Allies suffered accordingly, but realising their mistake would soon catch up.

The devastation that the machine-gun wrought on the battlefield had both a profound physical and phycological effect, causing future Prime Minister Winston Churchill, who had spent ninety days in the trenches of the Western Front, to write in a post war memoir, *"War, which used to be cruel and magnificent, has now become cruel and squalid."*

A plethora of different types of machine-gun appeared during the First World War and here I will list just a few.

Browning Machine Gun.

In 1900, John Moses Browning filed a patent for a recoil-powered automatic machine-gun and improved it in 1910 when he added a water-jacket to cool the barrel.

Although the gun worked well, he further improved the design by replacing the side ejection system with bottom ejection, added a buffer for smoother operation, replaced the hammer with a two-piece firing pin, and made some other minor improvements. The Browning entered service with the American forces in 1917 Fig 153.

Fig 153:   Browning machine-gun 1917

The Vickers Machine Gun

The British adopted the Vickers as its standard heavy machine-gun just before the start of World War 1. A water-cooled .303 based on the Maxim design, its chief drawback was its weight. At 83lb/37.7 Kg with its tripod, it required a crew of six to carry it Fig 154.

Fig 154:   The Vickers machine-gun 1915

The Marlin

Another gun that saw service with the Americans was the Marlin.

In 1917 the U.S. Army commissioned Marlin Arms to produce a version of the .30 Colt-Browning 1895 model machine-gun which was in use with the Navy Fig 155.

Fig 155:   The Marlin 1917

The Lewis Gun

The American Lewis light machine-gun entered the war with the British Army. Developed by U.S. Army officer Noah Lewis, the .303 gas-operated weapon was fed by a circular, top mounted, 50 round magazine and featured a distinctive "shroud" to cool the barrel Fig 156. The Lewis gun was widely used to arm Allied aircraft.

Fig 156:   The Lewis light machine gun.

The Chauchet

The French Chauchet had a bad reputation, mainly because some of the outer parts were of a poor quality and the crescent-shaped magazine had open sides that allowed mud and dirt to enter and jam the operation. Even when working well it had a slow rate of fire compared to other guns and the sights were frequently misaligned. Despite these difficulties it was nevertheless, the most common light machine-gun in service during the First Wold War Fig 157.

Fig 157:   The Chauchet

The Spandau

The German Spandau Fig 158, was a 7.92, water-cooled, belt-fed weapon, and it became the standard armament for German aircraft after the development of the "interrupter gear" that synchronised the weapon's firing rate with the revolutions of the aircraft's propeller, which allowed the gun to shoot safely through the arc of the plane's propeller.

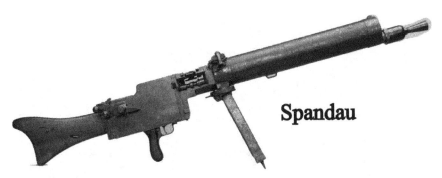

Spandau

Fig 158:   The Spandau

I have now taken you as far as I can go. This is not the end of the story of firearms by any means, it's just as far as I can take it. The development of the machine gun moved on after the First World War, and of course new types of weapons have been invented. Indeed, things have progressed so far from the days of the one on one battles between knghts and their battle axes, that man now has the ability to kill every living thing on the planet.

There have inevitably been gaps and ommissions in my story, as it would be impossible to cover everything in one book, but I believe I have covered all the main developments and advances up to the first world war. I leave you with a few oddities and other matters, to hopfuly cover one or two of the gaps, together with a gallery that shows some of the artistry that can be employed in gun making.

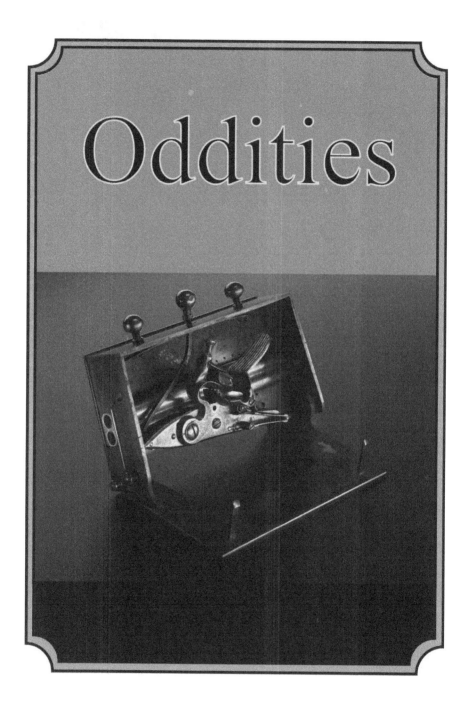

Oddities

Chapter 15

Oddities

Throughout the whole history of firearms, no matter what the prevailing lock or system of the time, there have been strange and unusual guns produced. Some have been pistols disguised as something else, some have combined two different types of weapon, some have been ingeniously concealed and some have just been downright bizarre. Here are just a few.

Sword-pistol

Fig 159: !8th century sword-pistol

Sporran clasp pistol

Fig 160 shows a Sporran Clasp of brass and steel with a concealed pistol inside which would fire if the sporran was not opened correctly. This may have inspired an episode in Sir Walter Scott's novel Rob Roy where the hero's sporran opens by twisting one button in one direction, another in another.

Fig 160: Sporran clasp pistol
National Museum of Scotland

One of the earliest bizarre weapons was the shield-gun shown in Fig 161. Henry V111 of England had several round shield-guns in his arsenal. The gun itself was unusual for the time, being among the earliest breech loaders to survive. The charge was loaded into a separate iron tube that was inserted into the breech, which pivoted upwards for loading and when closed was secured with a spring catch.

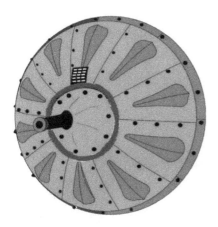

Fig 161: Drawing of a shield-gun

It is possible that these shield-guns were intended for use by special troops, perhaps a royal guard. The mechanism for firing them is a matchlock and one can only marvel at the ability and dexterity of the shooter. The shields are made of wood with a metal outer covering and must have been very heavy just to hold up, let alone load and fire.

When it came to firing, the shooter would have to hold the shield up so that he could see through the small grill just above the protruding barrel, aim at his target and then descend the serpentine into the priming pan. At such close proximity behind the shield, the flash from the pan must have taken its toll on eyebrows at the very least.

Bootleg Gun

Fig 162: Bootleg Gun

The top part of a boot that surrounds the leg has always been a convenient place to carry something concealed, illegal liquor for example or a weapon of some sort. The introduction of the percussion cap made the under-hammer gun much more practical and ideal for hiding in the boot.

Bicycle pistol

During early days of cycling one of the hazards faced was that of being harassed by dogs.

Protection could be provided in the form of a small blank firing pistol, such as the one shown in Fig 163.

Fig 164 is the type of advertisement that would appear in the small adds.

Fig 163: Bicycle pistol

THE · CYCLIST'S · FRIEND.

12/-   12/-

"I fear no tramp."

No Lady or Gentleman Rider should be without one. This lovely little shooter has Six Chambers, Ebony Handle, Folding Trigger, and is heavily Plated with Silver. Size, in length; easily carried in watch-pocket. Packed complete, with 50 Cartridges, Free by Rail, 12/3.
T. W. CARRYER & Co., Ltd., Gun Factors, Newcastle, Staffordshire.

These pistols were intended to scare the dog away by firing a blank round, and not to kill the animal.

Some advertisements would also be aimed at postmen who are notoriously at risk of a dog attack.

Fuse Igniter Pistol.

Fig 164 shows a Fuse Igniter Pistol, a Webley MK 1 1877 Model. Fuse Igniter Pistols were developed to allow demolition charge fuses to be ignited at a great distance. The cord was attached to the screw off barrel and a percussion charge loaded into the breech of the pistol to ignite the fuse when fired.

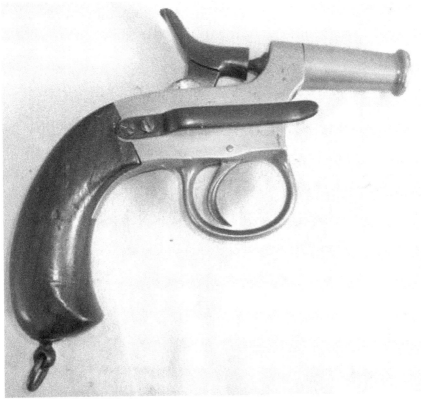

Fig 164:   Fuse Igniter Pistol.
J. C. Militaria

Knuckleduster-pistol

Among the strangest of combination weapons is the knuck-leduster pistol or "Apache," shown in Fig 165.

The knuckleduster or some form of it was known even back in Roman gladiatorial times, but the term knuckleduster only entered our vocabulary from American slang in the mid nine-teenth century.

The European Apache seems to have been named after a Parisian street gang, and was made by Belgian gunmaker Louise Dolne in the 1870s. It was a barrelless pinfire revolver with a spurless hammer, a folding trigger, a folding knife blade and a four-ringed knuckleduster that doubled as the revolver's grip.

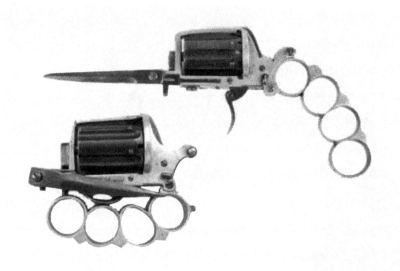

Fig 165:   The Apache combining a revolver, a blade and a brass-knuckleduster

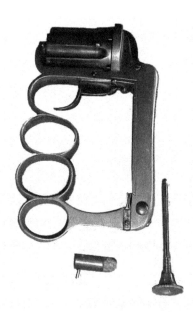

Fig 166:   Delhaxhe knuckleduster gun

The knuckleduster gun was popular throughout Europe until the early twentieth century and other versions were made by other manufacturers, notably by Delhaxhe, Fig 166.

The Delhaxhe design was obviously influenced by the Apache but had an open top frame and a fixed three-ring bow linking the trigger guard with the bar grip. When required the knife blade swivelled laterally to project beneath the butt.

The idea was briefly resurrected during the Second World War but was dropped so the money could be spent on more worthwhile projects. The design was a reworking of the Dolne model with a three-ring knuckle-bow, a folding trigger, a folding knife blade on the left of the frame, and an internal hammer. It was designed to take six 9mm parabellum cartridges.

Liberator Pistol

The liberator pistol Fig 167, was developed during the Second World War on behalf of the US Joint Psychological Warfare Committee and made by the Inland Division of General Motors.

Known officially as the "Flare Project," the Liberator was designed to be dropped behind enemy lines to arm partisans and resistance personnel.

Fig 167: Liberator Pistol

One million were ordered in 1942 at a cost of $1.710.000. Being only five and one-half inch long with a smooth bore, four and a half inch barrel, they were easy to conceal. Crudely made from stamped-out metal plates and spot-welded, there were ten .45 ACP cartridges hidden inside the hollow butt. The gun was operated by pulling the locking block back and turning it through 90° to the left.

This cocked the striker and allowed the breech block plate to be slid vertically to open the chamber. Any spent cartridge could be ejected with a separate ejector rod or even a long pencil, after which a new cartridge could be inserted into the chamber. The breech plate was closed and the locking block returned to its original position. The pistol was then ready to be fired.

The Palm Pistol

The protector pistol was a small palm pistol patented by Jacques-Edmond Turbiaux in France in 1882. It fired an 8mm centre-fire cartridge. Fig 168.

Fig 168: "Protector" Palm pistol

Fig 169 gives an idea of the size of the gun and shows the internal layout. Large numbers of these gun were made in France and later in America under the brand name "Protector."

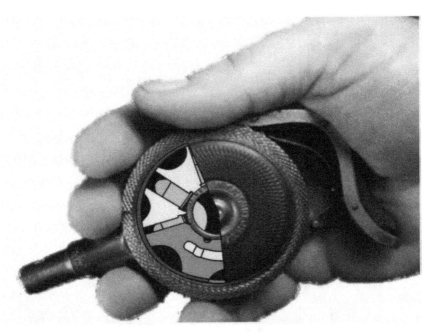

Fig 169: Cutaway view of a palm pistol

The palm pistols produced in America often featured improvements patented by Peter Finnegan of Austin, Illinois in 1893. The American gun was manufactured by the Ames Sword Company of Chicopee Falls, Massachusetts and was marketed first by the Minneapolis Firearms Company and then by the Chicago Firearms Company.

To fire, it was held in the palm of the hand with the barrel protruding between the shooter's fingers. The weapon was discharged by pressing a spring-loaded lever at the back of the frame against the palm of the hand. As can be seen in Fig 169 there were several projecting finger-spurs on the front of the

frame to assist with gripping the gun. The gun was loaded by
removing the side plate.

Turret Revolver

A revolver where the chambers are in a drum that is mounted
so that it rotates horizontally rather than around a horizontal
axis. This was done in an attempt to circumvent the patent
registered by Samuel Colt.

Chambers pointed in all directions, and the weapon was
prone to row ignition with all the chambers firing in sequence,
this often resulted in fatal accidents because one chamber
always faces the shooter Fig 170.

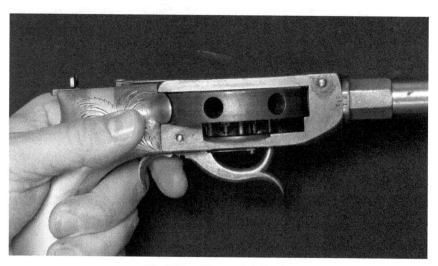

Fig 170:   Turret Revolver

Twenty Chamber Revolver

A very unusual revolver, firing twenty shots from a single cylinder and a folding trigger Fig 171. The pistol has an inner and an outer ring of chambers in the one cylinder and two barrels, each of which line up with one ring of chambers.

This is a pin-fire pistol and the hammer has two strikers, one above the other. The upper striker impacts the outer ring of cartridge pins and the lower striker the inner ring.

When the gun is cocked after firing a round from one of the outer chambers, the cylinder rotates only half the distance between two of the outer chambers so that when the hammer next falls, it is the lower striker that impacts with the inner ring of chambers and so on.

Fig 171:   Twenty shot revolver
Forgotten Weapons

Purse or Cigarette-case pistol

One way of concealing a gun was to house it in a metal purse or cigarette case as with the Frankenau purse gun shown in Fig 172, and dating from 1876.

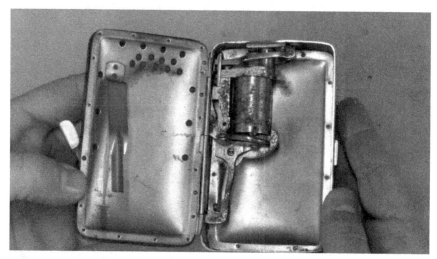

Fig 172: Cigarette-case pistol
Forgotten Weapons

Axe-gun

Another example of a gun being combined with different weapon is the Axe pistol that is shown Fig 173. In this case the axe is combined with a wheellock.

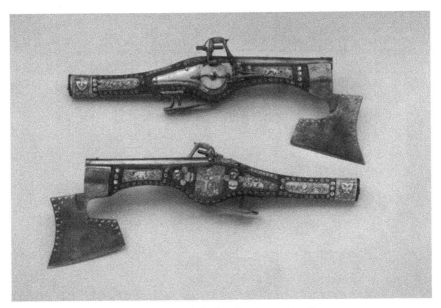

Fig 173: Pair of wheellock axe pistols.
Metropolitan Museum of Art

Other Matters

Chapter 16

Other matters

Making a barrel

A barrel is made by twisting a ribbon of iron around a core or mandrel that is of a smaller diameter than the required bore of the barrel. First the pig iron is placed in a "puddling furnace" where the impurities in the iron, that are generally lighter than the molten iron, float to the top where they are skimmed off.

Once the impurities have been removed the cooling iron is formed into square blocks, after which it is then pressed between rollers or hammered and formed into long ribbons. It is this ribbon that is heated and wound around the mandrel Fig 174.

When the spiralling was complete the edges were welded together by heating and hammering.

The next process was the boring of the barrel's interior to the correct size. This was achieved with a "bit" starting with a small bit and working up to the required diameter.

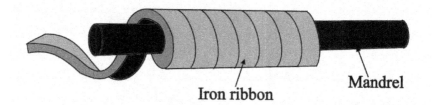

Fig 174: The ribbon was twisted around a mandrel

The barrel was cooled with running water during the boring process. Next the exterior was ground to shape. At first this was done by the barrel maker holding the barrel against a grinding wheel while slowly rotating it in his hands and then filing, but the process was later replaced with the use of a lathe.

The next process, if required, was to rifle the inside of the barrel. This was atchieved by having two cutters set in a rod that was attached to a spiral guide. As the cutters were pulled through the barrel they were rotated by the guide.

All that remained now was to close the end of the breech. In the days of the muzzle loaders this was achieved by simply screwing in a solid breech plug and drilling a touch hole close to the interior end. The introduction of Nock's breech plug superseded that method and the invention of the percussion cap saw even more changes.

With the advent of percussion systems the breech block, that was screwed into the end of the barrel, contained a cavity for the powder charge and a hole for the nipple to be fitted Fig 175.

It is often written that the iron for gun barrels was mostly obtained from old horseshoe nails because this was considered the best material. This may be true, or it may simply be that that they were an easy and plentiful source of iron, obtained from people who owned forges, which were also required for making barrels.

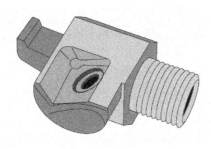

Fig 175: Percussion breech plug

Whatever the truth, one particular type of barrel was prized above all others and that was the Damascus barrel.

The Damascus barrel was made by taking almost equal proportions of refined iron and steel and welding them together into square bars. The bars formed in this way were then twisted by having one end secured in a clamp while the other end of the red-hot bar was rotated with tongs.

During this process the bars are watched carefully to ensure that they twisted evenly.

Three of these bars were then placed alongside each other, the centre one of which was turned so that the twist was of the opposite hand, and they were forged into a ribbon Fig 176.

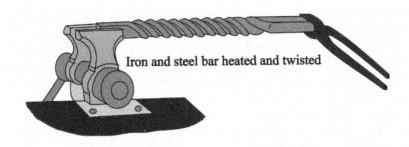

Iron and steel bar heated and twisted

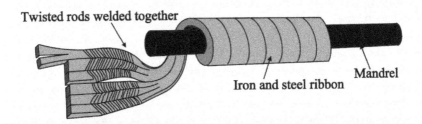

Twisted rods welded together

Iron and steel ribbon

Mandrel

Fig 176: Process of making a Damascus barrel

This ribbon was then coiled around the mandrel as previously described and the barrel finished and bored out as before.

Division of labour.

The barrel is of course only one part of an assembled gun, and it requires quite different skills to those needed to manufacture a lock or make a wooden stock and it would have been rare for any sixteenth or seventeenth century maker, other than perhaps a Court gunsmith or a particularly wealthy one, to have all the required kills assembled under one roof.

Until 1637, barrel makers would have belonged to the Guild of Armourers or Blacksmiths, the locksmiths to the Guild of Locksmiths and the stock makers to the Joiners' Guild. This division of labour means that the gunmaker's name that appears on the lock, may only have been the lock maker or gun finisher who purchase the parts from separate manufacturers. Barrel manufacturers would often apply their stamp or mark to the barrel, but that would mostly be on the underside where it would be covered by the gun's stock.

The exception to this was the practice of English barrelsmiths to stamp their mark on the upper side of the barrel. The English Gunmakers' Company that was responsible for proofing all barrels mounted up by London gunmakers, also applied their marks to the upper left side of the breech.

Proof marks

At first it was the responsibility of the Armourers and Braziers Company to prove gun barrels in England, but the practice does not seem to have really started until the London Gunmakers Company received its charter in 1637.

Barrels submitted to them were loaded with a double charge of powder and two balls. Several barrels at a time were fixed in a rack with the muzzles pointing towards a bank of sand and touched off by igniting a trail of powder which ran towards the touch holes. If the barrel withstood that test it was stamped with a V surmounted by a crown, meaning that the barrel had been "viewed." The barrel was then finished and tested again. If it passed this second test it was stamped with the letters GP surmounted by a crown, meaning, "Gunmakers Proof Fig 177.

A proof house was set up in Whitechapel, London, where a copper plate was kept upon which each gunmaker was required to stamp his mark.

In 1813 an Act of Parliament was passed establishing a central Proof House in Birmingham and decreed that all firearms made in both England and Wales must be proved by either London or Birmingham.

Fig 177: Proof marks

Powder and shot flasks.

Along with the introduction of the new firing system by Alexander John Forsyth and the development of the percussion cap, came gradual changes to the accessories that were supplied with the guns.

The old powder flasks of horn, bone or a dozen other materials Fig 178, were slowly replaced with ones made of leather or metal with stamped designs on them Figs 179.

Imaged by Heritage Auctions, HA.com

Fig 178: Typical powder horns

Fig 179: Metal powder flask from the percussion era

Shot flasks also become common in leather or metal and these usually had some device on the dispensing end to measure out the amount of shot required Fig 180.

Fig 180: A shot flask with measure

Expanding bullets

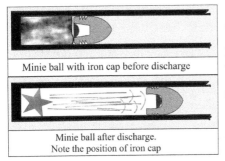

Minie ball with iron cap before discharge

Minie ball after discharge.
Note the position of iron cap

As mentioned in chapter five, Claude Etienne Minie refined Delvgne's expanding bullet and added a amall iron cap as shown below. It was later shown that the cap was dangerous and unnecessary and a new bullet designed by by James Henry Burton was adopted.

Cartridges

The Peabody Cartridge:

Peabody cartridge

A family of cartridges designed for use in guns of the Peabody-Martini design. Peabody cartridges include a variety of rare rimfires as well as some more common centrefires.

Pin-fire:

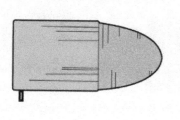

Pin-fire cartridge

A cartridge having a pro-truding pin, usually at right angles to the base of the cartridge and projecting through the side of the case. Impact of the hammer on this pin causes internal ignition .

Rim-fire:

Rim-fire cartridge

A major class of metal-cased cartridges which have the priming compound distributed in a ring around the base of the cartridge. The firing pin crushes the rim, igniting the primer.

Volcanic cartridge:

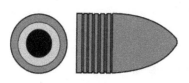

Volcanic cartridge

Cartridges designed for early Smith and Wesson (later Volcanic Arms) guns. They are deeply concave-based lead cartridges containing powder and primer within their bases.

They are an evolution of the Hunt Rocket Ball.

Wesson cartridge:

Wesson cartridge

A family of cartridges, many of which are rare and/or difficult to identify, designed for use in Smith & Wesson tip-up and other Wesson arms.

Paper cartridge:

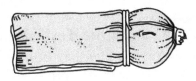

Paper cartridge

An early class of cartridge, usually consisting of a bullet and measured powder charge wrapped in a tubular paper envelope.

In use, the container was torn open, the powder poured down the muzzle of the weapon and the paper used as a wad or discarded.

Needle-fire:

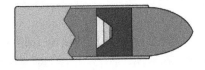

Needle-fire cartridge

A type of cartridge designed for use in a gun whose firing pin is a long needle-like device which penetrates the base of the cartridge and impacts upon a primer at the base of the bullet.

Linen cartridge:

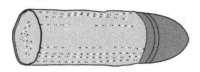

Linen cartridge

A combustible cartridge, usually for Civil War breech-loading long-arms such as the Sharps carbines and rifles. The powder was contained in a starched linen sack with a ni-trated paper base, which was fastened to the bottom of the lead bullet.

Extractor cord cartridge:

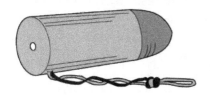

Extractor cord cartridge

A rare Maynard experimen-tal cartridge which utilizes a short length of cord to assist in extracting a spent case.

Buckshot, or shotgun cartridge:

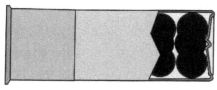

Buckshot cartridge

Generally, any cartridge loaded with a number of large round balls.

Originally the term related to deer hunting. The term has been applied to both old and modern cartridges.

Allen cartridge:

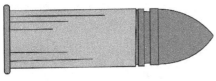

Allen cartridge

Ethan Allen was a gun-maker in the mid- 1800s who produced a distinctive series of cartridges along with his guns.

Boxer cartridge:

Boxer cartridge

Cartridge used in Snider rifles and generally adopted for English small arms after 1867.

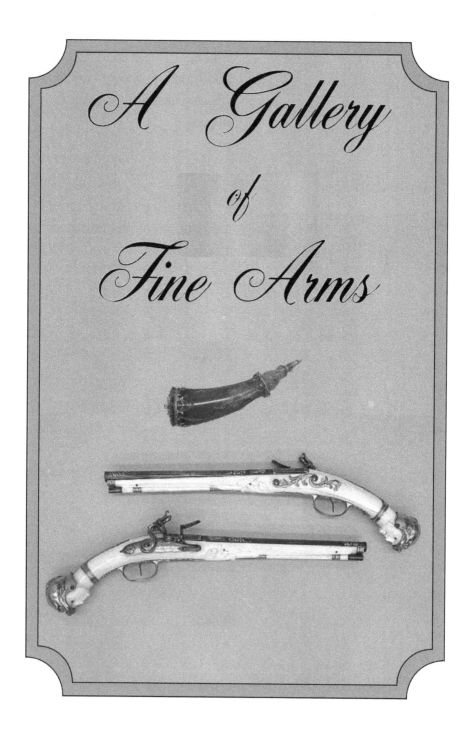

Gallery of Fine Arms

Courtesy of the Metropolitan Museum of Art New York

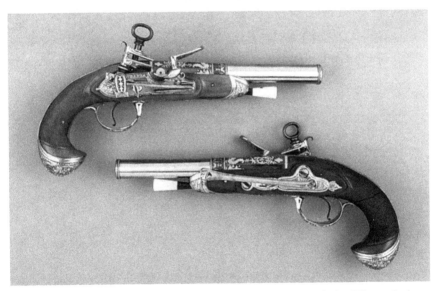

Spanish Flintlock pistols from the workshop of the Ybarzabel
family late 18th century

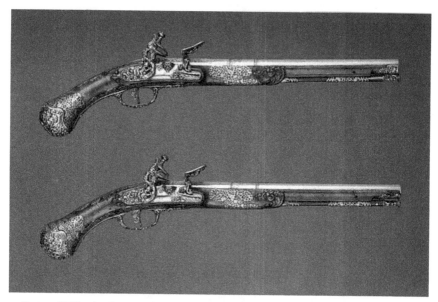

Pair of Flintlock pistols by Giovan Battista Franco, late 17th century

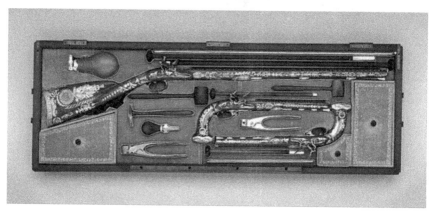

Cased rifle and pistols by Nicolas Noel Boutet, Vasailles 1800

Scottish snaphaunce pistol 1615 made for the Duck of Kurland

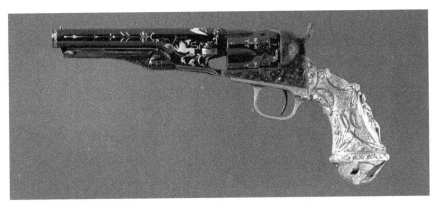

Colt 1862 Police model revolver in steel, copper and gold

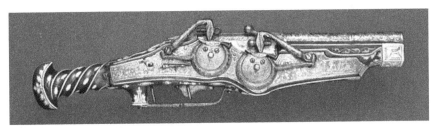

Doublr barrelled wheellock made for Emperor Charles V by Peter
Peck Munich 1542

Double barrelled shotgun with exchangeable flintlock or percussion
locks and barrels

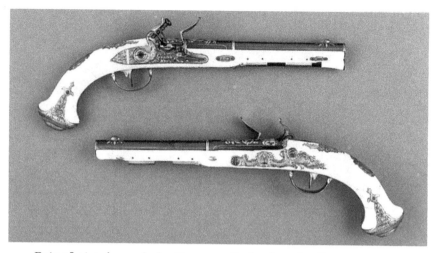

Pair of pistols made for Empress Catherine the Grear in 1786 by
Johan Adolph Grecke

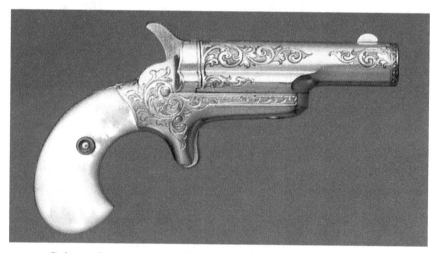

Colt pocket pistol c1870 in steel, gold, and mother-of-pearl

Turkish Miqulet rifle late 18th century. Steel. wood, ivory.
mother-of-pearl, gold, silver and glass paste

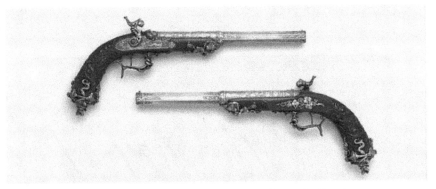

Pair of percussion target pistols made for the
1851 exhibition at Crystal Palace by Alfred Gaulvain
of Paris

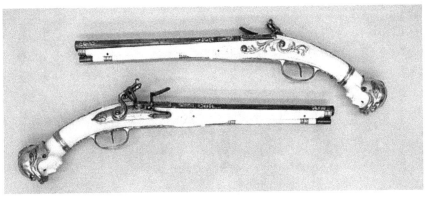

Flintlock pistols by Leonardus Graeff. Aachen, now Germany c 1675

Late 16th century powder horn in Amber, Gold, Enamel, pearls and
diamonds

A Glossary of Terms

Glossary of Terms

Accessory: Any article used with but not an integral part of the gun. Bullet mould, rammer etc.

Action: The assembly of moving parts that feed the cartridge into the chamber, lock and seal the chamber, fire the cartridge, unlock the chamber, extract and eject the empty cartridge case.

Action, bolt. The breech closure is achieved by longitudinal movement of the breechblock parallel to the axis of the bore. Types include turn-bolt action, straight pull action, camming-lug bolt and wedge-type bolt.

Action, double:
1: Firing mechanism in a revolver in which a continuous pull on the trigger will revolve the cylinder to place a cartridge in the firing position, cock and then release the hammer to fire the gun.
2: In some semiautomatic pistols, a mechanism whereby continuous pressure on the trigger cocks then releases the hammer to fire the first shot. Even so, the recoil from the first shot will cock the gun ready for the next, meaning that less pressure is required on the trigger for the second shot.

Action, lever: Breech closure is actuated by a lever linked to the breechblock in a manner that provides the desired opening and closing of the breech. Usually the lever is mounted under the receiver and forms a trigger guard.

Action, single: An action that requires manual cocking of the hammer before pressure on the trigger will fire the weapon.

Ammunition: Consists of the bullet or projectile, the propellant, the igniter or primer and the case. The current term for small-arms usage is cartridge.

Armory:

1.   A place where weapons are manufactured.
2.   A place where weapons are stored or displayed.

Arsenal: A place where ammunition is stored or manufactured.

Autoloading: Any of a variety of arms which, after being manually loaded and fired, will eject the fired case, load the next cartridge from the magazine and cock the gun ready for the next shot. Pressure on the trigger must be released and reapplied after each shot for the next shot to fire. Gas expansion, recoil and mechanical spring action are used to perform ejection and reloading operations.   Also called semi-automatic or self-loading.

Automatic: Any of a variety of weapons using gas pressure, recoil, etc. after the first shot is fired, to eject the fired case, load the next cartridge from the magazine, fire and eject that cartridge, and repeat the process continuously until ammunition is exhausted or pressure on   the trigger is released. The term is often misapplied to semiautomatic weapons.

Ball:

1.   A round lead or iron object discharged by a smooth bore firearm.
2.   Any spherical projectile.

Ballistics: Science of the performance of projectiles, relating to their trajectory, energy, velocity, range, penetration, etc.

Barrel band: Strip of metal encircling and fastening together the stock and the barrel. Also called a capucine.

Bell-mouthed: Flaring at the muzzle to scatter shot, as in a blunderbuss.

Bent: Notch or cut in machinery designed to catch on a lever.

Blade;   A type of upright, elongated front sight.

Blowback

1.   The normal reaction of powder gases backwards against
   the bolt or breechblock at the time of explosion and sometimes used
   to   operate the action.
2.   Rearward escape of powder or primer gases from
   the chamber around the bolt or breechblock caused by a split or
   fractured cartridge   case or a punctured primer.

Blunderbuss: Smoothbore firearm with a bell mouthed muzzle and
of large calibre.

Bolt: The part of the action that locks the mechanism during
discharge. In bolt action rifles it is the cylindrical block of steel that is
                pushed forward and locked to seal the breech
for firing.

Boot: Scabbard attached to a saddle to receive a rifle or carbine.
Bore: The hole extending longitudinally through the gun barrel
from chamber to muzzle. Formerly bore size designated a measurement
of   bore diameter in terms of the number of spherical
bullets that fitted the barrel, totalling one pound in weight.

Breech: The rear end of the barrel and more loosely, the related
mechanism of the chamber and receiver.

Breechblock: That part of the action which, being locked into position, supports the cartridge in the chamber of the gun, so that the case
may   form an effective gas seal when the weapon
is discharged. Although a bolt is a breechblock it is not normally referred
to as one.

Breech plug: In muzzle loading weapons, a cylindrical plug screwed
in at the breech to close the bore.

Bullet: The projectile discharged by a firearm.

Bullet, incendiary: A bullet containing an incendiary mixture or compound that generates intense heat on impact.

Bullet, tracer.:   A bullet containing, inside the jacket at the base of the bullet, a substance ignited on firing to show a brilliant light during its flight. It has an incendiary effect if flight is interrupted by impact before the light is exhausted.

Butt
1.   The rearmost face of the stock on a shoulder arm.
2.   The bottom of the grip on a handgun.

Buttstock: Portion of the stock extending from the receiver to the butt on a small arm.

Calibre: Distance across the bore measured from one side to the opposite side.

Cannelure: Indented ring or groove around a cartridge case or bullet with a variety of uses. Serving to either hold solid lubricant of a lead bullet, or to receive metal stripped from the bullet in passing through the bore, or to prevent the bullet from being pushed too far into the case, or to crimp the case to the bullet.

Cap: In ammunition it is a small metal or paper device containing percussion ignited compound designed to explode the main charge.

Carbine: A shortened rifle or musket, usually with a barrel length less than 22 inches and adapted for use by mounted troops.

Cartridge: Any of a variety of metal containers holding a complete charge of explosive, including primer powder and bullet. Formerly cartridge described powder contained in paper which was inserted into the chamber by pouring the charge through the muzzle. As such it dated from the end of the 16th century. Though paper cartridges contained no ignition component, they provided faster loading and better protection from dampness. Current metallic cartridges fall into several categories depending on the shape of the base and the type of ignition device.

Cartridge, blank: A blank cartridge has no bullet, with a wad inserted instead to retain the powder.

Cartridge, centre fire: Normally made of brass, aluminium or steel with the primer contained in a small metal cup in the centre of the cartridge base.

Cartridge, rim fire; Made of soft ductile metal, often copper, wherein the priming mixture is inserted in the rim at the head of the case and can be detonated by the blow from the hammer or firing pin at any point on the circumference of the rim.

Cartridge, rimless: Since a rim interferes with automatic feeding, either a rimless cartridge or a cartridge with a very small rim (semi-rim) is used in automatic weapons, a grip for the extractor being provided by a groove just above the base of the case. All rimless cartridges are of centre fire type.

Cartridge, rimmed: Characterised by a rim or flange around the base to prevent the cartridge from entering too deeply into the chamber, to sustain the blow of hammer or firing pin, and to provide grip for the extractor. Such cartridges may be either rim fire or centre fire.

Chamber: The enlarged rear end of the barrel that receives and supports the cartridge, aligning the bullet with the bore and the primer with the firing pin.

Choke: The bore of a shotgun barrel, the inside diameter of which is smaller at the muzzle than at the breech, designed to compress or constrict the load of shot in its travel through the barrel so that it leaves the muzzle in a more compact mass

Clip: Metallic cartridge holder to facilitate loading into repeating small arms.

1. Mannlicher clip: A clip that is inserted into the magazine along with the bullets and is generally ejected after the last round has been fired,
2. Clip Stripper clip: A clip that is removed before the first round is fired.

Cock
1 On a flintlock weapon the hammer or piece holding the flint.

2   On percussion weapons, the piece striking the cap, also referred to as the hammer.

3   To draw back the hammer or firing pin against mainspring compression in preparation for firing a weapon. At full cock the trigger mechanism engages the hammer or firing pin, holding it against mainspring tension, so that pressure on the trigger will release the hammer or firing pin, causing the mainspring to drive it against the primer to fire the weapon. Half cock arrangement on some firearms permits engaging the hammer in a notch or bent, far enough to the rear to prevent accidental firing of the primer. In this case trigger pressure will not fire the gun. In some revolvers half cock frees the cylinder to turn for loading and unloading.

Cocking stud: Part of the cocking piece, a projection engaging the trigger or sear to hold the firing pin in the cocked position.

Comb: On a shoulder arm, the ridge at the upper forward part of the buttstock, used as a grip.

Cone: On a percussion firearm, the tube on the end of which is placed the cap containing fulminate or other priming compound. When the hammer strikes the cap on the cone the resultant detonation sends a flash through the tube to ignite the charge. Also called a nipple.

Contreplatine: Plate or scroll of metal inlet into the stock of a gun opposite the lock. Though sometimes purely ornamental, it can also serve as a washer for the screws holding the lock in position. Also called a side plate or nail plate.

Cordite: A nitro-glycerine propellant, so called because of the powders cord-like shape. Is was used principally in Great Britain.

Cylinder: On a revolving type firearm, the mechanism holding a number of cartridges and moving about an axis in such a manner that successive charges are correctly aligned and locked in position for firing.

Damascus: On a barrel, it refers to a kind of steel or iron displaying a peculiar marking or "watering" produced during manufacture. Originally from the 10th century, such steel was brought from India and Persia to Damascus, which at that time was the main junction for trade between East and West. The weapons, however, were not manufactured in that city.

Dog lock: Variety of flintlock, probably of Moorish origin, though used in Britain in the second half of the 17th century. On the rear of the lock plate a pivoted hook can be made to engage with a similar hook on the rear of the cock to act as a safety.

Ejector: On breech loading small arms, a device that removes the empty cartridge case after firing.

Extractor: Device for withdrawing a cartridge case from the chamber.

Ferrule: Loop fastened below the barrel to carry a cleaning rod or ramrod.

Firing pin: The part of the firing mechanism which by striking the primer, explodes the propelling charge. Some firing pins are an integral part of the hammer or striker, some are mounted separately within the hammer's forward face, some are separately attached to the striker's forward end. Some are constructed as distinct units mounted in the bolt or standing breech, capable of moving forward when struck and of recoiling when the primer fires.

Flask: Any case, either of horn, wood, leather, shell or metal designed to carry and often measure and dispense a powder charge.

Flint: A piece of silica capable of fracturing to a sharp edge and of producing sparks when that edge is struck against steel. Clamped into a flintlocks hammer, the flint creates sparks by striking the metal frizzen.

Flintlock: Mechanism igniting a firearm's charge by the sparks that are produced by striking flint against steel.

Forestock: On some muskets and rifles, the forward part of the stock extending from the trigger guard forward under the barrel.

Fouling: Foreign matter in the bore of a firearm, the term refers to gummy matter, burnt powder grain and light rust. Heavy rust is generally te
rmed corrosion rather than fouling.

Frame: Of a pistol or revolver, the receiver or non-movable forging that houses the firing mechanism, magazine, cylinder, etc. In hinged frame revolvers the frame consists of the grip section, the lock-work section, and an extension above the trigger at the forward end of which the barrel and cylinder are hinged. Frequently the term frame is applied only to revolvers, corresponding roughly to the receiver of an automatic pistol.

Frizzen: Also called the battery, it is part of the firing mechanism on a flintlock arm. A pivoted piece of steel (iron with a steel face) against which the flint strikes to produce sparks for igniting the priming powder. In pre-percussion days the frizzen was sometimes called the hammer. European frizzens are generally smooth. Oriental frizzens are almost always ribbed vertically to provide a more efficient igniting instrument.

Frizzen spring: The U-shaped spring on a flintlock designed to hold the frizzen either erect over the pan to keep it covered or tilted forward to u
ncover the pan at the time of firing.

Fulminate of mercury: An explosive compound capable of ignition if heated, vibrated or struck. Discovered by Howard in 1800, it has in the past been extensively used as a detonator for less sensitive explosives, though now fulminate has been largely replaced by more stable priming compositions.

Gatling gun: An American machine gun consisting of a cluster of barrels circled about an axis which were revolved, loaded and fired continuously by winding a crank handle.

Grip:
1 On handguns it is the portion gripped by the hand firing the weapon, often improperly called the butt.
2 On shoulder arms it is that portion of the stock immediately behind the breech

Gun: Any weapon firing a projectile. Originally the term harquebus meant gun, though later it became confined to a light and ornate weapon used by the wealthier classes for sport. The term musket was used to designate the military arm as distinct from the sporting gun. Until the term rifle, musket or a variant of that word continued to signify any type of gun that was a standard military arm. A caliver was a military arm lighter than a musket but of larger calibre. The haquebut was a very light gun, only a little larger than the early pistols. The petronel was still smaller with a peculiarly curved stock for firing from the breast. use.

Gunpowder: A propellant mixture, discovered in Europe in the early 13th century, composed of saltpetre, hardwood charcoal and sulphur. Coarser grained powder generates nearly the same muzzle velocity with much less pressure than finer grains. Since 1700 the composition of all powders has remained substantially unchanged, though powders differ greatly in grain size. Early powders were mechanically mixed to form black powder. Present powders are compounded chemically.

Half bent: The first or half cock notch in the tumbler of a gunlock.

Hammer: On a flintlock it was the piece hit by the flint but in subsequent locks it was the striking piece, corresponding to a flintlocks cock. In modern usage a hammer denotes a pivoted mechanism, that moves about an axis to deliver its impulse to the firing pin. A hammer may be visible or contained within the guns frame (hammerless). Its action may carry the firing pin directly into contact with the primer, or it may impel a separate firing pin forward against the primer. A burr hammer denotes an exposed hammer with a serrated gripping surface. A spur hammer denotes any hammer having a protruding cocking spur. A straight line hammer is found on certain guns like the Smith and Wesson Straight-line in which the hammer drives straight forward when released from the cocked position. On a revolver the hammer is usually exposed for cocking, though on some pocket models the spur is omitted.

Hand cannon: Any of a variety of small crude cannon dating from the early 15th century and adapted for individual use by fitting wooden stocks to rest against the shooters chest, arm or shoulder. The hand cannon was the prototype of all subsequent shoulder arms.

Hand gun: A pistol or revolver.

Hang fire: A delay in firing or a failure to fire, a delayed ignition of the powder charge after the hammer or striker has been released. Very dangerous as there may be several seconds between when the firing pin strikes the primer and when the weapon discharges.

Harquebus, Arquebus: Originally a smoothbore matchlock introduced in Germany in the mid 15th century. The term harquebus which means "gun with a hook" persisted through wheellock and flintlock designs. By the late 16th century the name harquebus had been superseded as a descriptive term by musket.

Heel: The upper rear corner of the butt.

Holster: A leather or web carrying case for a revolver or pistol to be carried about the person.

Horse pistol: Any of a variety of large pistols formerly carried by horsemen.

Jacket: The hard metal covering surrounding the lead core of a bullet.

Kick: The sum of recoil components in a firearm as felt by the shooter

Land: In the bore of a firearm, the uncut portions of the surface left after the grooves have been cut into the metal to form the rifling.

Lanyard: A cord attached to the butt of a pistol or revolver and used to attach the weapon to the user's wrist.

Loading gate: In revolvers, a hinged portion of the standing breech, provided only on weapons with cylinders that do not swing clear of the standing breech for loading.

Lock:
1 The firing mechanism on muzzle loading weapons.
2 On breech loading weapons, the firing mechanism and the mechanism designed to lock the barrel against the standing breech.

Locking lug: On a firearms bolt, one of several machined projections designed to engage in corresponding recesses in the receiver to hold the breech securely closed during the discharge of the weapon.

Lock plate: On percussion and earlier firearms, the external metal plate on which the firing mechanism is mounted.

Machine gun: A weapon firing small arms ammunition on the automatic principle at a high rate of fire.

Magazine
The operating assembly holding a number of cartridges to facilitate loading for successive discharges. The cylinder of a revolver is a magazine, though the term is never applied.

Mainspring: The spring actuating the striker or hammer of a firearm.

Matchlock: Mechanism for igniting a firearm's charge by bringing a lighted match into contact with priming powder in the pan.

Miquelet: The earliest Spanish flintlock, deriving its name from the robber bands of Catalonia who used the weapon.

Musket, Mousquet: Originally, a smoothbore small arm invented about 1540, much heavier and more powerful than the harquebus.

Muzzle: The end of the barrel from which the bullet leaves the weapon.

Muzzleloader: Any firearm only capable of being loaded through the muzzle.

Needle gun: First rifle using bolt action, invented by Nicholas Dreyse and adopted by the Prussian Army in 1841. The primer, placed against the bullet beyond the powder, was detonated by a needle passing through the powder when the trigger was pulled. In theory combustion was thereby maximised.

Nipple: In percussion weapons, the cone.

Ordnance: Collectively, military supplies, especially weapons, ammunition and related paraphernalia.

Over and under pistol: A firearm, usually of the hinged frame type, with two or more barrels placed one over the other.

Pan: Of a matchlock, wheel lock or flintlock gun, the receptacle for holding the priming charge.

Patch
1   Of a muzzle loader, a wrapping of leather, cloth or paper, usually greased, placed over the muzzle of a rifle when a bullet is rammed into the rifle to provide a closer fit between the bullet and the bore.
2   On high velocity ammunition, a hard metal jacket encasing the lead core of a bullet to minimise lead fouling, to improve the bullets ability to take the rifling, to flatten the trajectory and to maximise accuracy.

Pawl: Lever with a catch to engage in a notch or bent.

Pepperbox: A handgun characterised by three or more barrels grouped around a central axis. Popular in the mid-19th century, pepperboxes vary greatly in size and number of barrels. Most used the percussion system.

Petronel, Petrinal, Poitrinal: A post medieval hand arm, generally hung about the neck on a lanyard and fired with the appropriately shaped butt end flush against the chest. Intermediate in size between an arquebus and a pistol, the weapon was short, heavy and of large calibre.

Pistol: Loosely, any weapon designed to be fired by one hand. In this sense revolvers are included.

Prime: To prepare a weapon for firing by placing a primer or priming powder in a position suitable for igniting the main charge.

Primer: The device that detonates when struck, igniting the propellant charge of a cartridge.

Primer Maynard: The Maynard primer was a variant of the percussion cap and resembled the caps in a child's cap pistol. Pellets containing explosive were sealed at appropriate intervals between two strips of paper. The resulting tape, having been rolled, was inserted into firearms designed to receive it and cocking the hammer brought a pellet into position over the ignition vent leading into the chamber.

Pyrites: Metallic sulphide, a mineral possessing the property of producing sparks when brought sharply into contact with steel or iron. Pyrite was used to produce sparks in wheel lock and early flintlock weapons. Flint had more suitable qualities for ignition and eventually superseded it.

Rammer: Loosely, a ramrod.

Ramrod: Of a muzzle loader, a rod employed in loading the weapon by ramming the wad and bullet or shot down the barrel.

Receiver:
1   Of a rifle, the metal housing to which the barrel is attached and in which the bolt mechanism, the magazine assembly and the trigger assembly are contained.
2   The frame of an automatic or semi-automatic pistol.

Recoil: The rearward motion immediately after discharge caused by expansion of powder gasses

Revolver: Hand gun with a fixed barrel and revolving cylinder composed of chambers holding ammunition.

Revolver, double-action: A double action revolver is designed so that repeated trigger pressure both revolves the cylinder and cocks and releases the hammer to discharge the piece. Such weapons are often designed to allow manual cocking as well.

Revolver, single-action: These require manual cocking of the hammer, trigger pressure will not cock the weapon. Manual cocking revolves the cylinder to align a chamber with the bore and cocks the weapon. Trigger pressure then releases the hammer to discharge the weapon.

Ricochet: In ballistics, a bullet which strikes a surface and glances off.

Rifle: A long barrelled gun, the bore of which carries longitudinal spiral grooves to impart spin to the bullet in flight.
Rifle, repeating: Also referred to as a magazine rifle and is capable of discharging several rounds with a single loading of the magazine contained in or attached to the weapon. Extraction and reloading are however performed by hand.

Rifling: The grooves cut into the bore of a firearm to impart rotary motion to a bullet for gyroscopic stabilisation.

Safety: Any mechanism designed to prevent accidental firing. The mechanism may be a lever, button or slide.

Saltpetre: One of the three components of black powder.

Sear, or scear: Pivoted latch in the firing mechanism, operated by the trigger and designed to hold the firing pin or hammer at full or half cock until released.

Serpentine: Of a matchlock firearm, an "S" shaped lever, pivoted in the middle. A slow burning match is inserted into the upper portion so that pr essure on the lower portion (trigger) will bring the match into contact with the priming powder in the pan.

Setscrew: On a firearm, a screw designed to regulate the pressure required to release the trigger

Shell:
1   Any projectile propelled by a powder charge.
2   In small arms ammunition, an empty metallic cartridge case.

Shotgun: A smoothbore shoulder arm designed to fire shells containing numerous small shot as projectiles.

Side-arm: Any arm designed to be carried on a belt at the side when not in use, including swords, bayonets, pistols and revolvers.

Silencer: A device attached to the muzzle of a firearm to reduce the noise of discharge.

Slide: In semiautomatic pistols, the metal sleeve covering the barrel and top of the action, driven rearward by recoil and returned by spring action. The slide ejects the fired case, cocks the firing mechanism and feeds a fresh cartridge into the chamber.

Sling: On a shoulder arm, a leather or web strap attached to the weapon to assist in carrying the gun and also used to steady it during firing.

Smoothbore: A rifle with an unrifled bore, such as musket, blunderbuss etc. Also sometimes used to describe a shotgun.

Snaphance, Snaphaunce: An early flintlock invented in the Spanish Netherlands (Holland) simultaneously with the miquelet in Spain. The action is similar to later flintlocks except that the pan cover is manually operated. Dating from the 16th century the system may derive its name from a Dutch word meaning "chicken thief"

Solid-frame: On a revolver, an unhinged frame. Loosely a revolver in which cartridges must be ejected singly, or in which an axis pin must be withdrawn before the cylinder can be removed from the frame.

Stock: The wooden part of a shoulder arm, attached to the receiver, by means of which the weapon is held, aimed and fired. Sometimes the stock may be made of metal, plastic or other rigid material. The quality and design of stock is of great importance in increasing the weapons accuracy.

Striker: A rod like firing pin moving within the bolt or breechblock and actuated by its own spring when released by the trigger. The striker moves straight forward in line with

Throat
1   Of a firearms chamber, the forward section tapering to coincide with the diameter of the bore.
2   Of a revolver, the bore's enlargement at the breech end, designed to centre the bullet in the barrel as it jumps from the cylinder when the weapon is discharged.

Tige: Formerly in rifles, a steel pin in the breech against which the ball, hammered by the ramrod, was made to expand to fit the grooves of the bore.

Touchhole: In early firearms, a hole at the rear of the barrel, through which the powder within the barrel was lighted by means of a torch applied externally.

Trigger: Any of a variety of devices which, by acting on a sear, causes the firing mechanism to discharge the weapon.

Trigger, double set: Constructed as a set of spurs, is arranged so that pressure on one spur engages the sear in a manner that permits the second trigger to discharge the weapon with very light pressure. The arrangement is common on sniper weapons and on match target shooter weapons.

Trigger, folding: Quite common on pocket pistols in the 18th and 19th centuries the trigger is hinged to fold forward in a recess beneath the frame, bringing the hammer to full cock causes the trigger to spring forward ready for use.

Trigger, set: A set trigger is designed to operate with very light pressure. Set triggers are normally adjustable and are sometimes called hair triggers.

Trigger, sheath: Denotes a trigger recessed to project from the frame just forward of the grip. It requires no trigger guard.

Trigger guard: A loop frame partially protecting the trigger from damage or from unintentional pressure that would accidentally discharge the weapon.

Vent: Any small hole, channel or tube designed to conduct the flash of the priming powder from the breech to the main charge in the chamber.

Very-pistol: A weapon designed to discharge flares for signalling purposes.

Wad: A piece of paper, cardboard or felt used to retain the charge in the cartridge or barrel.

Wheellock: Mechanism igniting a firearm's charge by sparks produced by holding pyrites against a rapidly revolving serrated wheel. The system was devised in the first quarter of the 16th century and employed on both hand and long arms.

Index

Other book by Colin Holcombe

Samuel Colt   The Man Behind the Gun   ISBN: 978 1787 234031

The Story of Flight   ISBN: 978 1527 267626

The Theory of Flight for the Layman   ISBN: 978 1716 465390

The Great Race   Britain to Australia 1919   ISBN: 978 1527 289673

Born in Post War Bristol
From Bomb Sites to Test Flights   ISBN: 978 1399 931922

Printed in the USA
CPSIA information can be obtained
at www.ICGtesting.com
CBHW052116210124
3647CB00011B/962